The Podcaster's Audio Gu

The Podcaster's Audio Guide is a concise introduction to simple sound engineering techniques for podcasters. This digestible guide explains the basics of audio engineering, from equipment, to recording, editing, mixing and publishing. Suitable for beginners from all backgrounds, including students and hobbyists, as well as professional content producers looking to experiment with podcasts, *The Podcaster's Audio Guide* is the perfect resource with cheat sheets, starting set-ups and a comprehensive jargon buster.

Jay Cockburn is a sound engineer, podcast producer and journalist. He worked for the BBC in London for eight years before moving to Toronto, where he produces podcasts for big brands like Canada's biggest newspaper *The Globe and Mail*, HSBC and the Toronto Maple Leafs. He is also lead producer on Darts and Letters, a podcast about radical thought and progressive ideas.

The Podcaster's Audio Guide

Jay Cockburn

Routledge
Taylor & Francis Group

LONDON AND NEW YORK

Cover image: Georgia Webber

First published 2022
by Routledge
4 Park Square, Milton Park, Abingdon, Oxon OX14 4RN

and by Routledge
605 Third Avenue, New York, NY 10158

Routledge is an imprint of the Taylor & Francis Group, an informa business

© 2022 Jay Cockburn

The right of Jay Cockburn to be identified as author of this work
has been asserted in accordance with sections 77 and 78 of the
Copyright, Designs and Patents Act 1988.

British Library Cataloguing-in-Publication Data
A catalogue record for this book is available from the British Library

Library of Congress Cataloging-in-Publication Data
Names: Cockburn, Jay, author.
Title: The podcaster's audio guide / Jay Cockburn.
Description: Abingdon, Oxon ; New York, NY : Routledge, 2021. |
Includes bibliographical references and index. |
Identifiers: LCCN 2021045437 (print) | LCCN 2021045438 (ebook) |
ISBN 9780367495541 (hardback) | ISBN 9780367495534 (paperback) |
ISBN 9781003046578 (ebook)
Subjects: LCSH: Sound—Recording and reproducing—Digital
techniques. | Sound—Recording and reproducing—Equipment
and supplies. | Podcasts—Production and direction. | Acoustical
engineering. | Digital media—Editing. | Podcasting.
Classification: LCC TK7881.4 .C625 2022 (print) | LCC TK7881.4
(ebook) | DDC 621.389/3—dc23/eng/20211110
LC record available at https://lccn.loc.gov/2021045437
LC ebook record available at https://lccn.loc.gov/2021045438

ISBN: 978-0-367-49554-1 (hbk)
ISBN: 978-0-367-49553-4 (pbk)
ISBN: 978-1-003-04657-8 (ebk)

DOI: 10.4324/9781003046578

Typeset in Times New Roman
by codeMantra

Contents

Figures

1   Introduction

Welcome to podcasting properly

Podcasts are easy to make, right?

Sort of.

It's easy to record two people chatting about your chosen topic into a phone or laptop, put it on the internet and call it a podcast.

At one point that might have been enough. Plenty of shows are variations on that. Dan Harmon's *Harmontown* is essentially a 90-minute, multi-person ramble with a bit of Dungeons and Dragons thrown in.

But like the early DJs coming ashore from Radio Caroline, podcasting has evolved. That scrappy show is competing against the BBC, Spotify, NPR and the *New York Times*. These are huge institutions with professional studios, sound engineers and teams of producers. They're making science fiction dramas, daily news shows and true crime epics… and all of these are made with teams of professionals who have made a career out of knowing what to do. Gimlet's *Crimetown* feels like watching a high budget TV drama – and with good reason, *Crimetown* was made by former HBO producers.

We are way past the days of podcasting being just the audio version of a blog. Podcasts are a rapidly growing form of storytelling that is picking up the baton from public radio. Podcasts are proving that interesting stories that are told well and presented effectively are incredibly popular.

The investments being made into podcasts are huge. Spotify is building content creation hubs in New York, Los Angeles, London and Mexico City.

There are a limited number of listening hours in a day and your podcast is competing for them. Listeners aren't going to be more forgiving just because your show was made by two people in a bedroom. There isn't much room for a podcast of dodgy quality any more.

If you want loyal listeners, you need to step up your game and get to grips with sound. You have to understand the equipment you're working with and how to manipulate and shape your recordings into something beautiful and easy to listen to.

Luckily, it's still pretty easy to make great sounding podcasts. You don't need hundreds of thousands of dollars worth of set design, lighting

DOI: 10.4324/9781003046578-1

and cameras. You just need a couple of good microphones, a laptop with software and this book. The barriers to entry are still much lower than film and TV. A bedroom or garage can be co-opted into a podcast studio with a little creativity (and lots of blankets).

So, welcome to this crash course into audio production for podcasts.

By the time you finish reading this guide, you'll have all the tools you need to turn your ideas into a professional sounding podcast. You'll understand how to create that sparkling quality you've come to expect from shows like 99% Invisible and The Daily.

If you already have a podcast, then you'll find out how to make it stand shoulder to shoulder with the industry's heavy hitters.

If you're feeling a bit overwhelmed by all the different buttons and settings in your software and you just want to know what setting to choose, then this book will feature cheat sheets that you can use as a starting point... By the time you've read this book, you'll be comfortable setting up your software, but these will save you some time if you just want to start making stuff quickly.

We know you've got ideas and content covered, and with so many exciting and creative ways to make a podcast this guide isn't going to tell you what to put in your show. What it will tell you is how to make whatever you do sound like you've got a team of producers, sound designers and engineers helping you.

We're going to start with gear, and even if you already have your kit it is worth reading through the chapter on equipment as it will help you understand what you already have and how to use it best. The goal here isn't for the book to tell you what to do, it's for you to understand what you need to do and why you're doing it.

After that the guide will cover recording techniques, editing tricks and nailing that final mix. Then, we'll turn that final mix into a master copy and show you how to get it out there onto the internet and in people's headphones.

There are some technical standards to adhere to which make sure your show sits well alongside the other shows on places like iTunes and Spotify. They can seem daunting but loudness standards are actually super simple, so we'll tell you how to get your show in line with them.

By the time you've finished this book, you'll be able to confidently approach a wide range of situations and show formats and walk away with a great sounding podcast that you can publish proudly.

If you're looking to get your first foot in the door of making a career out of podcasts, then tape syncs are one of the first freelance gigs a lot of producers will pick up. Follow the exercises, and by the time you finish, you should be ready to pick up those quick and easy jobs which help you make those crucial connections at production companies. Remote recording without ever going into a studio has become much more common too, especially during and after the COVID-19 pandemic, so those essential skills are all part of becoming a pro producer. Remote recording can save on studio costs and is easier logistically, so it's not going anywhere.

The podcast landscape is richer than ever, the industry is growing and people want to get involved. Let's get a head start on them.

The stuff you need to know first

The commandments of podcasting

Get your recording right because no amount of editing or noise reduction software can completely fix bad audio.

Brief your guests properly because most people don't know proper microphone technique. If you are recording remotely, this could mean doing test recordings.

Always over-prepare by bringing too many batteries, testing your microphones and cables and having backup recordings running.

The stages of making a podcast

- **Development**: creating your concept. This might include doing some market research, crafting a show mission statement or a style guide and show bible.
- **Pre-production**: planning your recording by booking interviewees, finding locations and choosing your gear.
- **Gathering material**: recording your audio, whether in a studio or in the field.
- **Editing**: starting with a content edit, then a technical edit, then a final edit.
- **Mixing**: balancing all the audio to make sure everything is at the right levels and then processing it to make it sound as good as possible.
- **Mastering**: creating a master copy of the show, ready to publish.
- **Publishing**: putting it out there for your adoring fans.

Some basic knowledge you need before we get started

There is going to be some technical language here but don't worry, you really don't need to properly understand the physics of it all. This is here because it can be helpful to understand a little of the terminology we're going to be using. Don't worry if you don't get it on the first read. These terms will pop up throughout the book but you can just skip back here if you need.

Frequencies

Sound is a spectrum, just like colour in light. This spectrum is measured in Hertz (Hz) and KiloHertz (kHz). 1kHz is 1,000Hz.

The human ear can, at its best, hear between 20Hz and 20,000Hz, so for making a podcast, or any audio, that range is all you need to worry about. As we age, we naturally lose the ability to hear the upper end of that spectrum, so in reality you don't need to worry as much about frequencies over about 13kHz.

Unless you're making podcasts for cats.

We'll talk in more depth about different parts of the frequency spectrum, but for now you need to know that lower frequencies are associated with bass and higher frequencies are treble.

If that means nothing to you, then picture yourself in a loud venue – maybe a nightclub or a concert. You can hear all of the music because you are right in the heart of the venue. Now, you need the bathroom – what happens to the music as you close the door behind you? It muffles but you can still hear a part of it. The walls and door of the bathroom have removed the higher frequencies, or the treble, leaving just the boomy vibrations of the bass frequencies.

The lower end is the weighty, deep reverberations you can feel. The higher end of the spectrum is the clarity and sparkle.

If you are interested in learning more on this, then here is a little bit more on the physics: sound is created by variations in air pressure, and Hertz refers to "cycles per second"; so if a sound is a pure tone wave of 100Hz, lasting exactly one-tenth of a second, then that variation in pressure has occurred ten times (Figure 1.1).

In reality sound is made up of combinations of different air pressure changes at different frequencies. We can use equipment and software called an EQ, or equaliser, to emphasise and de-emphasise certain frequencies and tailor our sound. In fact, all the equipment you use will have subtle effects on how frequencies are represented.

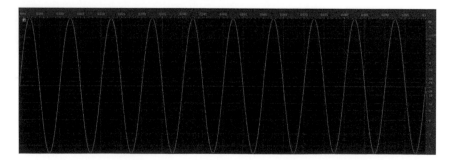

Figure 1.1 100Hz.

DeciBels

We measure how loud a sound is in deciBels (dB).

There are different forms of deciBel but what you really need to know is that for most software the highest possible volume will be 0dB, with the metre usually reading down to about −60dB, or for total silence, infinity. This is because digital signals are often measured in "deciBels Full Scale" (dBfs).

Generally, you want your signal to be as close to 0dB as you can get while leaving some headroom so that big peaks don't go over. If your signal goes above 0dBfs then it will clip, or distort. You don't want this; it sounds bad because by overloading the software you lose important parts of the signal... this is called clipping, more on that later.

Hardware may measure in deciBel volts (dBv), because it is measuring the intensity of an electrical signal. These measurements can go above 0; however, you may still introduce a form of clipping.

dB are logarithmic, meaning that 8dB is not double the loudness of 4dB. Perceived loudness does not increase in a linear fashion.

For podcast production, you don't need to know about the maths involved, but it's helpful to remember that an increase of 10dB sounds like the loudness has doubled.

Sample rate

The short version: the higher this is, the better the file's sound quality. Never work under 44,100Hz (usually written as 44.1kHz).

The long version:

When analogue audio is converted to digital audio, it is turned into a series of samples. Each sample measures the amplitude of a signal at a point in time, so that it can be reconstructed as it plays out. The more samples that are created, the closer to the original analogue signal the digital version gets.

In order to accurately reconstruct a sound wave, it needs to be sampled at least twice per cycle (this is known as Nyquist's Theorem). Humans can hear up to 20,000Hz, so we need to sample at least 40,000 times a second. That's why you will see most people working at the standards of 44,100Hz and 48,000Hz.

Bit depth

The short version: a higher bit depth will give you more dynamic range – that's the difference between louder and quiet. This means you get a better ratio of signal to noise. Never work under 16-bit. Most audio professionals work at 24-bit.

The long version: each sample that is taken of an audio signal when turning it into a digital file contains a certain number of bits. The more bits per sample, the more information can be stored. As each of these samples is measuring amplitude at a point in time, increasing the bit depth allows for a greater variation in amplitudes, therefore a higher dynamic range.

Unwanted noise is often low level, so having a higher bit depth allows that noise to remain low level. If you have a low bit depth, that noise will be brought up to the point that you can easily hear it interfere with your signal.

If you save a mix as an 8-bit WAV file, it will have noticeable hiss. The difference between 8-bit and 16-bit is pretty stark, so make sure you're working at 16-bit or higher. 24-bit is very common. 32-bit is probably excessive for podcasting.

Clipping and distortion

Clipping is what happens when an audio signal is too loud for the equipment or software it is running through. The top of the waveform gets "clipped" off, becoming a flat line. This creates distortion, which is usually unpleasant to listen to.

Producers and recording engineers spend a lot of time and energy avoiding clipping. We'll go into this in more depth in Chapter 3, but for now I'll just say keep your signals below 0dB.

2 Equipment

Introduction to equipment

There is no "right" set-up for making a podcast. The gear you use is a personal choice. Every selection you make will affect what you record, how your recording process plays out and ultimately how the show sounds. What works for you might feel clunky and awkward for another podcaster.

Choosing your equipment is a creative choice, as well as a technical one. Everything you use affects the sound. Equipment can even affect the content too by changing the way guests interact. Choosing gear that is uncomfortable to work around isn't going to get you the best interview.

So there is no right set-up for making a podcast, but there are plenty of wrong ones. Your beautiful studio quality microphone is going to sound great recording voice-overs in a studio, but if you are making a podcast that involves collecting a lot of audio outside, it just isn't going to work.

So I'm not going to tell you what to buy, because it could be wrong for you and because manufacturers are releasing new equipment all the time. It's far better to have the knowledge you need to make your own decisions.

I am going to tell you what you need to know so you can make your own choices and create your own set-up that works for what you want to create.

You've probably already seen the gear marketed towards podcasters. Attractively cheap USB microphones that promise to do away with the need for a complex and expensive rig... and sometimes that Blue Yeti is exactly what you need, but if you're looking to make your show sound like the real deal – and want to have some more fun recording it – then you can get much better results by knowing your gear, whether renting, buying or just hopping into a university or library studio. We're here to teach you when to go for that USB mic and when to switch it up with some professional grade gear.

You've probably already got a computer, but it is such an important part of the production process that we're still going to cover what is important for audio editing, including where a really small investment

DOI: 10.4324/9781003046578-2

could supercharge your processing power. The software you use is important too, and there is a whole range of different suites for different budgets. To get the most out of this guide though, and to stay in line with industry standards, it's recommended you use Adobe Audition.

This is only a guide.

Really knowing what works for you is something you learn by playing around with bits of different kit. Get acquainted with your local audio rental spot and try some stuff out! There is an endless amount you can learn just by having some fun recording stuff.

Microphones

A Microphone. A tool for converting sound waves into electricity. Sounds simple... it kind of is simple, but is one of the most important choices you'll make during production.

Perhaps the one thing that affects your final sound the most is the microphone that you choose. If you're planning on rigging your own space into a studio, your microphones will probably be your biggest expense, and unfortunately it's an area you really shouldn't cut corners. You're the artist and the microphone is your instrument.

If you're on a budget then there are options. I would always recommend hiring gear to test that you like it before investing in it.

If you want to save money in the meantime there are options. For a simple interview format podcast, some public libraries have basic podcast studios you can use for free – Toronto Public Library has several, for example.

However, by the end of this chapter, you'll be equipped with the knowledge you need to choose the right microphone for the right situation, whether you're hiring, purchasing or working with a studio.

The key part of a microphone is the diaphragm. That's the tiny bit of metal behind the grill. Sound waves vibrate this diaphragm and it converts the waves to an electrical signal, just like the eardrum connected to your auditory nerve.

The first thing you want to know about any microphone is what type of mic it is. Most microphones fall into one of two categories.

Condenser vs dynamic

Pretty much every microphone you encounter will be either a condenser or a dynamic. There are others (notably ribbon microphones), but you're pretty unlikely to encounter those when making a podcast.

You will probably find yourself using condensers more than dynamic microphones – I certainly do, but there are lots of reasons to use a dynamic mic too.

Condensers are generally more sensitive, especially to higher frequencies, so your in-studio voices are going to sound crisper and your field recordings will pick up those little bits of atmospheric sound that liven things up.

The downsides are that condensers tend to be a little more fragile and more expensive, which is why when you watch a live band you will almost always see that energetic singer chucking a dynamic microphone around.

A condenser's sensitivity is a two-edged sword. In noisier environments condensers will pick up more background noise, so if you are going to record interviews in a space with lots of unwanted background noise, then perhaps a dynamic mic would be a better choice.

Note that I said "unwanted" background noise there. Not all background noise is bad; it can add colour and dynamism to your recording as long as it isn't overpowering the speech. Learning how to work with and accommodate for this type of mic's sensitivity is an important part of working with them.

They also need power – this is what that +48v button is for on your other recording gear, so you'll burn through batteries a little quicker when you're recording out and about. This is known as "phantom power" and is fed through the audio cable. There's no need to plug it into the mains; however, not all interfaces will be able to provide phantom power.

Pros

- More sensitive than a dynamic
- Better at capturing higher frequencies, so voices will sound crisper

Cons

- More sensitive than a dynamic
- Requires power
- Costs a little more money
- More fragile

Where you might use a condenser

- Recording speech in a controlled environment such as the studio
- Gathering field audio
- Recording acoustic instruments

Dynamic microphones are also a very useful tool in the podcaster's microphone arsenal.

Dynamic microphones are less sensitive, so they are really useful in environments with more ambient noise that you don't want to pick up.

The signal a dynamic microphone puts out is lower, so you'll need to make up for that by applying more gain further down the recording chain (we'll talk all about gain in Chapter 3, when we get to actually recording stuff). However, dynamics are usually better than condensers at handling very loud sounds, so you'll often see them on guitar amps or being chucked around by shouty lead singers.

Dynamic mics also don't need power, so there is no need to worry about that +48v switch.

You can pick up the classic workhorse mic, the Shure SM58, for around $100. The Shure SM58 is probably what you think of when you picture a microphone. It's incredibly durable and versatile, deals well with handling noise and sounds pretty good on voices.

When I say durable, I mean there are videos of people throwing SM58s off of buildings and then using them to record afterwards. An SM58 will keep working to −100C, although your other gear probably won't.

If you're on a limited budget and just want a couple of usable microphones, then dynamics will serve you well – just don't expect them to sound quite as crystal clear as a more expensive condenser. That doesn't mean that dynamics are inherently worse than condensers; far from it. They're a different tool for a different situation and an arguably more versatile one at that.

Pros

• Better in loud environments with lots of ambient noise
• Cheaper
• More durable
• Doesn't require phantom power

Cons

• Less sensitive
• Often poorer response to high frequencies

Where you might use a dynamic

• In a room with loud ambient noise such as appliances or air conditioning
• A crowded space with lots of people talking in the background
• In adverse weather conditions

Polar patterns

The second thing you want to know about the microphone you're using is the polar pattern. That's just a technical term for which directions the mic picks up sound from. There will usually be a diagram looking a little like this on the mic itself, usually close to where the cable plugs in. Some microphones give you an option of a variety of polar patterns which can be changed with a switch on the microphone itself (Figure 2.1).

I find it helps to picture different microphones as different attachments on a garden hose, spraying the water in broader or narrower jets depending on which one you pick.

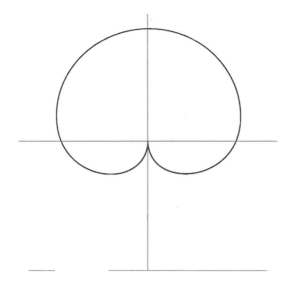

Figure 2.1 An example polar pattern.

The sounds you don't want to pick up are the things you don't want to get wet... so keep those in the dead zones.

Of course, water gets everywhere when you're hosing stuff; so if you really don't want something included in the splash zone, its best to keep it as far from your microphone hose as possible.

Omnidirectional

Often shortened to "omni". In theory, these pick up sound in a sphere around the diaphragm – that's the bit inside that picks up sound waves. In reality they're usually still going to pick up sound better in the direction you point the microphone, especially at higher frequencies.

An omnidirectional mic will have a polar pattern diagram that looks something like this (Figure 2.2):

These diagrams are only a rough approximation of what a polar pattern actually means in practice. In reality the microphone picks up sound in a three-dimensional pattern; so in the case of an omni mic, it would be a sphere. Due to the way sound disperses and the existence of reflections those areas that show as dead zones are never truly dead.

Omni mics are great for recording field sound, as you can hold them quite loosely and still pick up a nice amount of your voice while having a nice lively recording, rich with lots of atmospheric noise. They're also often used in classical music recordings to pick up the natural reverberations of a performance space.

You usually aren't going to want to use these to record your voice-over or guest interview in a studio (or other recording space) as you'll also

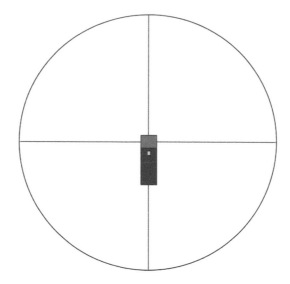

Figure 2.2 Omni polar pattern.

pick up a lot of reverberations from any flat surfaces. That doesn't mean you should never use them for interviews though. Perhaps you are recording in a space that has a lovely acoustic to it, such as a church, and you want to make sure the recording reflects that space.

It is possible to use omnidirectional mics with a lot of success to record interviews, for example, walking through a space while talking. It won't sound like a studio recording, but in this situation you probably don't want it to.

Tip

Higher frequencies sound waves emanate in a more directional way than bass frequencies, so even with an omni directional microphone a voice is going to sound crisper if the mic is pointed towards the mouth.

Cardioid

This is a roundabout way of saying "it picks up sound mostly in one direction and less in the other". The actual pattern of sound capture is heart shaped (Cardio-id. Get it?) (Figure 2.3).

Cardioid is probably the most common polar pattern on mics used on a voice. It allows for a speaker to move around a little in an interview but still records in only one direction. It's directional but forgiving.

There's a dead zone behind the microphone, making a set up of two cardioid mics especially useful for one-on-one interviews.

You pronounce it "cardy-oyd".

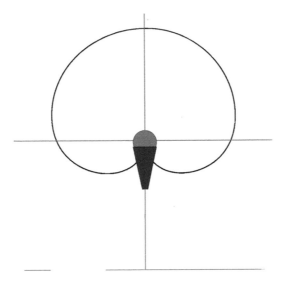

Figure 2.3 Cardioid polar pattern.

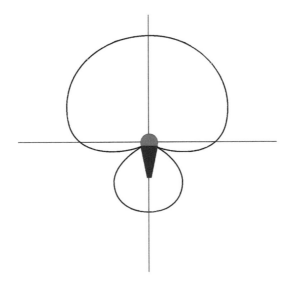

Figure 2.4 Hypercardioid polar pattern.

Supercardioid and hypercardioid

As you've probably worked out, these are more directional than a cardioid microphone, with the added quirk of picking up a small area directly behind the microphone due to how they work. These are best if you want to avoid picking up stuff to the side of the microphone (Figure 2.4).

It's probably best to avoid these in a studio setting, because often in an interview with two speakers the other speaker will be directly behind the microphone, so you would get a lot of bleed. They can be really useful when you're out in the field though, especially if you're working with a lot of background noise. Just remember about that "lobe" on the back of the polar pattern. If you're holding it and making a bunch of noise yourself, it is going to get picked up!

Bidirectional or "Figure 8"

These mics pick up equally in two directions – front and back of the microphone.

This can be a workaround for a two-person recording if you only have one microphone, but that is going to make mixing and balancing much more difficult. Both people will be on the same track with no way of separating them (Figure 2.5).

You're far better using two separate mics than trying to record two people with a bidirectional mic.

However, you might want to use this, if you are looking for a microphone that is almost omnidirectional but doesn't pick up as much sound to the sides of the microphone.

Remember that polar patterns are three-dimensional!

It really does help to think of the microphone like the attachment on a garden hose. It's tough to represent a polar pattern on paper because it

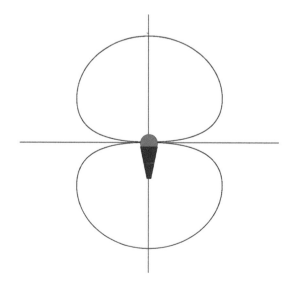

Figure 2.5 Bidirectional or "figure of 8" polar pattern.

is a three-dimensional thing, so a truly omnidirectional microphone will pick up all sounds equally in a sphere around it, whereas a truly bidirectional microphone will pick up sounds in two spheres on either side.

Some other types of microphone

Shotgun

Most professional podcasters will have one of these in their field kit (Figure 2.6).

If a microphone is a hosepipe and the cardioid polar pattern is what you use to water the plants… then the shotgun mic is the attachment you use to spray your friends with a concentrated jet of water. These are great for picking up sound from a specific source in less than ideal conditions, so they're great to have in your kit if you're going out to record in the field.

Figure 2.6 Shotgun mic.

You need to be very conscious when handling these though – they have the same quirk as super/hypercardioids and pick up directly behind the capsule. The narrow pickup field is also pretty unforgiving, so you need to be really conscious of your mic placement and keeping your arm steady.

Lavaliers

Lavalier mics or clip mics are the kind you'll see newscasters and meteorologists on the TV using. They clip on to clothing relatively discretely, so they're particularly popular for recordings that are being filmed. They're usually omnidirectional to make up for the fact that they're not going to be pointed directly at the source of a person's voice (Figure 2.7).

You can use these for podcasting; in fact, they're great if you have a particularly animated guest. They are very expensive for quite a niche use though, and if you're not filming, you will get better results from other microphones. You need to watch out for clothing that rustles a lot too. It's very possible to ruin a recording with a cheap suit or sports jacket!

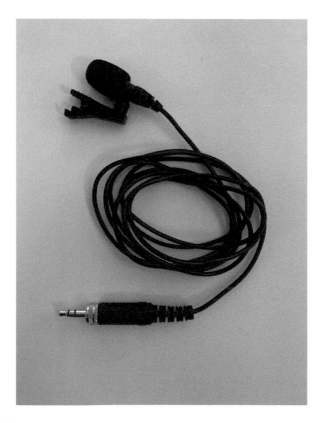

Figure 2.7 Lav mic.

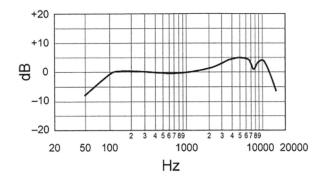

Figure 2.8 Example frequency response chart.

Frequency response chart

If you're looking to buy, rent or just using someone else's microphone, then there will likely be one of these in the case with the microphone – usually as part of the manual.

All pieces of equipment have an effect on the final sound, but the microphones have an especially noticeable effect. This chart shows which parts of the frequency spectrum are emphasised or diminished by a particular microphone. It will look a little like the example below (Figure 2.8).

This chart is the frequency response for a Shure SM58. It shows that the microphone picks up frequencies evenly between 100Hz and 1,000Hz, emphasises frequencies between 2,000Hz and 6,000Hz as well as 7,000Hz and 9,000Hz, but doesn't pick up frequencies above 10kHz well. It also doesn't pick up frequencies below 100Hz very well. This is actually a really good frequency response chart for speech.

You should definitely look at these charts before picking a microphone, but there is no substitute for just trying out a microphone and seeing how it sounds. There are subtleties that can't be shown on a chart.

The Shure SM58: the workhorse mic

In general, this guide will avoid recommending specific microphones, but I am going to make an exception for the Shure SM58 (Figure 2.9).

The SM58 is one of the most durable and most versatile microphones you can buy and it's only around $100. It's a dynamic microphone that actually sounds really good for the price. Every podcast producer and sound engineer will have at least one of these in their kit and if you're on a tight budget, it is a solid bet for a first microphone.

The 58 is a real workhorse microphone. With its cardioid polar pattern, it is great for recording speech, and the frequency response chart

Figure 2.9 Shure SM 58.

shows that it lifts the frequencies associated with clarity in the human voice. It's not as great at recording ambient sound and it will never have the sparkling high end of a really expensive condenser, but if you are looking for a good first purchase you can't go wrong with an SM58.

USB?

If you're on a really tight budget, then USB microphones can seem like a good option. Most microphones connect via Ground, Left, Right (XLR) cables – and most computers don't have an XLR input.

Using a traditional mic is not as simple as just buying a cheap cable end converter, like you would with some types of signal. If you want to know why... well, an audio signal starts off analogue – an electrical signal is carried from the microphone down the cable to a piece of equipment which will convert it to a digital signal that a computer can understand. This "analogue to digital converter" is usually an audio interface or a handheld recorder. We'll cover both of those later in this chapter.

USB microphones allow you to skip buying an audio interface or handheld recorder, which would have that important XLR input. The mics are often pretty cheap themselves – usually under $200. They work this way because they have the analogue to digital converter built in to the microphone.

You can get some USB mics that sound great – the Blue Yeti, despite its questionable name, is THX certified and a professional quality piece of kit. You can select different polar patterns, and I know of some radio hosts using these to broadcast from home when they can't get into the studio. A USB microphone is a really convenient piece of equipment to have and set up.

However, you have to jump through hoops to record two mics at a time, so you're going to really limit yourself by going USB. Without special software and awkward driver setups, your computer often thinks that multiple mics are just one mic, resulting in both audio streams recording to one track.

When you do eventually switch away from one USB mic and invest in some proper audio gear, then your USB kit becomes nearly useless.

The USB makes these mics vulnerable to electrical interference, usually in the form of clicks and pops on your recording. These are often quite easy to remove with noise reduction software, but it is always better to get a quality recording in the first place.

If your project only requires one microphone recording at a time and you don't intend to scale up your gear later, then sure, go ahead and buy a USB microphone. Otherwise it is worth a bit more money upfront for more flexibility.

Besides all that, we are looking to be professional audio producers here, right? So why not aim for professional grade gear and get yourself some proper XLR mics if your budget allows it.

Some companies, such as Shure, are now releasing mics that work as both a USB mic and XLR mic.

That said, USB mics are easy to use and quick to set up and lots of podcasters have a lot of success using them.

Some common situations

The studio interview

Scenario: you are interviewing a guest on your podcast in a relatively quiet room. It has a little echo, but not too much.

Solution: as the room is good, I would pick **two condenser microphones** with a **cardioid** polar pattern. Preferably something with a large diaphragm and grill that is designed for recording voice in a studio. In a professional studio setting with top-end equipment, you would likely be using something like a Neumann U87 here or the BBC favourite: the AKG C414. AKG also makes a cheaper microphone that is similar to the C414 – the C214, which is pretty good too. But you've read this chapter now, so you don't need me to tell you exactly which microphone to pick! You can understand the user manuals and make an informed decision yourself.

The noisy walk around

Scenario: you're going to a noisy street festival and want to narrate what you see while walking around, possibly interviewing some people if you find an interesting guest.

Solution: take one shotgun microphone and one omnidirectional microphone. The shotgun is highly directional and can record yourself talking without picking up too much background noise. You can record any interviews by moving this one microphone between yourself and the guest.

The omni mic is there to pick up atmospheric noise (or "wildtrack"). You'll probably want it to be a nice sensitive condenser that has minimal handling noise. You could also use this mic as a second mic for your guest, recording to two separate tracks.

The Beyerdynamic M58 is designed for news reporters in the field and is a pretty good low budget option here.

Note how I have suggested a setup that gives you multiple options for how you record here. Flexibility is important. It is best to go into a recording situation with an idea of how you are going to record, but with the ability to pivot if it is not working.

Field recording and handhelds

Lots of podcasts are made entirely in a studio and recorded directly into a computer, but if you're making anything other than a straight conversation you're going to want atmospheric recordings and actuality... all that wonderful colour that elevates a podcast above just people talking.

Luckily, it is really easy to gather your own audio, and it makes podcast production way more fun. It can take a bit of time, but ultimately you'll be lifting your show from a conversation to a story.

Plus if you are going to pick up work as a tape-sync, then you'll definitely need some recording equipment. More on that later.

In a pinch, do it on your phone

Smartphones are everywhere.

If you have a smartphone, you already have a recording device. It isn't the best – they are designed to be stuck to the side of your head after all, but if you find yourself caught unawares or you just don't have the budget for a proper handheld recorder yet, then a smartphone is better than nothing. You might be surprised how many big name podcasts get their remote guests to record themselves into their iPhones.

Even if you do have a proper handheld recorder, then get familiar with your phone's recording function. On an iPhone, this is called "Voice Memo". On Android phones it is called "Recorder". Get comfortable with the app! This will also come in useful when you inevitably want to record someone remotely and can't get a tape-sync to them (more on that later).

Learn where your phone's microphone is so that you don't accidentally cover it with your hand.

Wind noise can be a problem, but a quick and easy hack is to use a thin sock or pair of tights as a wind shield.

If your phone's app supports it (Android's recorder does), then record to WAV format. This is the highest quality.

Of course, you're still recording into a phone so it is never going to be perfect, but it might grab you something that you wouldn't have got otherwise. Podcasting's roots are pretty DIY, so it is fine to embrace that from time to time.

But get a good handheld recorder

Again, I'm not going to tell you which to buy. I'm going to tell you what to look out for when shopping around.

Reliability is key. When you have recorded that killer interview or grabbed an incredible chunk of audio from the field, you do not want to get home and find out that your files are corrupted. It's worth buying from reputable brands. Tascam, Zoom, Edirol, Rode, Marantz and Sound Devices are all reputable manufacturers of handheld recording gear.

That's not an exhaustive list – just a few examples of well-known companies that make these devices. The important thing is to do some searching and check out reviews of these products to make sure they aren't known for breaking down, and when you are in the field have fresh batteries (and spares) as well as enough space on your device's storage.

These are the key things to look at when choosing a recorder:

Inputs and outputs

Sound goes in the input and comes out the output! You need these to plug in microphones and headphones.

Does it have an XLR input? If so, how many? This is the standard way of plugging a microphone into your handheld recorder, so you will want at least one to plug an external microphone into. If you are recording an interview, then two are needed to accommodate the extra microphone. Perhaps you want even more than that for more complex recordings. Make sure you have enough inputs for your needs (Figure 2.10).

For outputs, consider who wants to hear the recording as it is going on. Are you the producer? You should definitely be listening and checking for audio quality, but does your host feel more comfortable hearing themselves? If so, they'll need a second headphone output.

You probably know the standard output as a headphone socket. Remember iPhones had them once upon a time? Well a smaller recorder might have one of those, but they might also have a bigger version of the same thing. Don't worry if it doesn't fit your headphones, you can get adaptors for these sockets very easily. It is exactly the same cable just with a different sized jack on the end. The technical term for this is a Tip

Figure 2.10 XLR input with cable.

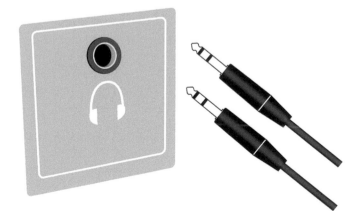

Figure 2.11 TRS output with cable.

Figure 2.12 Hybrid input.

Ring Sleeve (TRS; if you look at the pointy bit, you'll notice it is split into these three sections) (Figure 2.11).

It's not that common to have more than one or two headphone outputs; so if a lot of people need to hear what's going on, then consider buying some kind of splitting equipment.

Many handheld recorders now have inputs that accept both XLR and large TRS connectors. They look like this (Figure 2.12):

Internal microphones

Does it have them? If so, how many? It's always useful to have a microphone built into the recorder in case you find yourself without a mic or a cable has died. This is pretty common in handheld recorders.

The internal microphone is unlikely to be as good as having external microphones plugged into the recorder, not least because you remove a lot of flexibility when it comes to positioning as well as removing the ability to use different mics for different situations.

Almost all handheld recorders will have one or two microphones built in to make mono or stereo recordings, respectively. Make sure you know how to switch between mono and stereo if you are going to use these and which of the mics is used when recording in mono.

Button and handling noise

This is easily overlooked when you are trying out different hardware recorders, but do the buttons make a noise when you press them, and if so does it appear on the recording being made? You don't want to have to change some settings while recording and have a load of button clicks recorded all over that killer interview which you have travelled especially to get.

A lot of recorders come with a helpful "mark" button as well, which lets you put timecode markers on the audio as it is recorded, which can be really helpful during the edit... unless hitting that mark button makes a big click and ruins the part you wanted to mark. The first recorder I ever owned did exactly that.

Similarly, is there handling noise? Some of the more poorly built recorders have parts that aren't secured too well and if you move them while recording they can cause clicking sounds on your audio. You really don't want to be limited to setting your recorder down in one place... sound can create movement, but not if your recorder is stuck to a table. Make sure you check handling noise with mics and cables plugged into the recorder as well. If the cable connection is a little loose then that can be a problem.

Storage

This is where your audio is saved. Most recorders take some kind of SD card, so check if it comes with one and if not... go get a couple!

Internal storage is useful, in case you lose your SD cards. It isn't absolutely necessary, but it's good to know if it is there.

If you are recording in stereo at CD quality (WAV format, 16-bit depth and a sample rate of 44.1kHz), then you need roughly 10mb of storage per minute of audio. So, 1 gigabyte (GB) of storage gets you just over 1.5 hours of recording time. A lot of professional production companies work at 24-bit, 48kHz and that needs about 17mb per minute of audio recorded, meaning 1GB gets you an hour of audio.

File formats, bit depth and sample rate are all explained in Chapter 1 Part 2, but don't worry if you haven't got your head around it. As long as your bit depth is set to 16-bit or higher and your sample rate is 44.1kHz or higher, then you are almost certainly recording at high enough quality.

Most recorders have some kind of USB connection allowing you to plug them straight into your computer when extracting audio, but it is worth checking in case you need to get a card reader for your computer as well.

Setting your recorder up

Every recorder has a different menu system but they mostly have variations on the same options. A lot of what you are doing is balancing storage space against recording quality.

Recording settings

These settings are usually found in the recorders menu, in a submenu titled "Rec Settings" or similar:

- **Mono or Stereo** – It's tempting to think of stereo as "left and right", but really it just means there are two channels of audio being recorded. If you are recording with two microphones, make sure you are set to stereo. If you are just recording with one microphone, then switch to mono (aka one channel) to save space. For safety, I usually leave my recorder set to stereo. It's easy to mix a stereo track down to mono but you can't split mono back out to stereo. It's usually the "left" or "channel 1" microphone which will be recorded when set to mono, but check first!
- **Mic Power** – This might also be labelled **+48v**. This is phantom power for condenser microphones. Turn it on if your microphone needs it, but turn it off to save battery otherwise.
- **Low Cut** – Your recorder might have the option to cut frequencies below a certain frequency, for example, 80Hz. This can be used to avoid ground rumble from, for example, a road or footsteps. I usually leave this off as it can be easily applied in editing with a bit of equaliser (EQ), and I would rather capture the bass frequencies and then remove them if I want than not have them in the first place.
- **Format** – Usually various qualities of WAV and MP3. Avoid recording straight to MP3 unless you are getting really short of space and don't have any other option. It's best to avoid repeatedly compressing audio, so starting with high-quality WAVs is good practice.
- **Autogain** – Quite a lot of recorders come with a function that sets the gain automatically. If you're a novice, this is a good way to avoid most clipping (also known as overmodding or distortion).

These settings are usually found on the recorder's default, "home" screen ready to use while recording:

- **Gain** or **Rec Level** adjusts the level of the audio going in to the recorder. This is really important! If you set it too high, then you will get clipping, also known as overmodding or distortion. Bad clipping is impossible to reverse fully and will ruin your recording. Similarly, if the record level is too low, then there will be a very poor signal-to-noise ratio, creating a hissy and difficult to salvage piece of audio.
- **Volume** or **Playback Level** sets the level of the output, therefore your headphones. Start low, and try not to blow anyone's ears off.

- **Record** is usually not a one-button press. Often hitting record once "arms" the record, so you start hearing the microphones on your headphones and allowing you to set your gain and volume levels. You'll then have to hit either record again or play, depending on your recorder.
- **I'm sure you didn't buy this book to be told what the "Play" and "Power" buttons do...**

Other functions

- **Format** – OK I understand this is confusing, but the word for completely wiping your storage is "formatting" it. This is because traditionally this allows you to change the storage format, although most recorders just do the wiping part. It's good practice to do this before heading out as it reduces the risk of data corruption... just make sure you've taken all the files you need from the card before you do it!
- **Hold** – If none of the buttons are responding on your recorder, it is likely the hold switch is on. This is often a little sliding switch on the side of the recorder which deactivates all the other buttons to stop you accidentally stopping a recording or having the recorder turn on by mistake in your bag, for example.

I know I said I wouldn't tell you what to buy, but there is one recorder that is pretty much the industry standard, so if you skimmed everything above and want to get straight to buying some kit, then check this one out:

Zoom H4N

Price: $220–$250 (Figure 2.13)

Zoom has dominated the handheld recorder market recently and this model is a staple of podcasters and broadcast journalists. I've seen more people use this particular recorder than any other, and with good reason. It's relatively sturdy with rubber shock proofing. It's a really flexible piece of gear while remaining pretty simple to use. The price isn't too high either. There are cheaper recorders out there but they're cheaper for a reason.

It can also record up to four tracks of audio at once, which is pretty unusual in a handheld of this size. The H4N achieves this by allowing you to record two external microphones at the same time as the two internal microphones, so it isn't a great way to record extra guests but more of an

Figure 2.13 Zoom H4N.

option to get room noise or atmos while also recording an interview or a very rough musical recording.

The inputs are hybrid XLR (for microphones) and TRS or jack for recording from something at line level, for example, a live talk that had already gone through a mixing desk.

The onboard preamps are good quality for their size and price too, introducing a relatively small amount of noise.

Other common handheld recorders

Tascam DR-05

Price: $100–$130 (Figure 2.14)

If you're on a really tight budget and just need to get hold of something you can record with, then this is a low budget option. It suffers from handling and button noise, and you need an adaptor to plug an external microphone into the one mini TRS input, but otherwise it is a perfectly serviceable recorder.

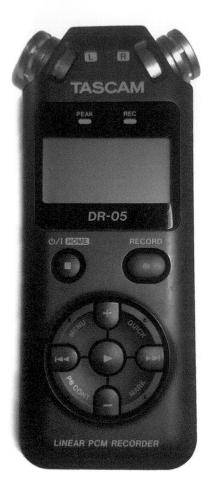

Figure 2.14 Tascam DR-05.

Marantz PMD 661

Price: $270–$320 (Figure 2.15)

Marantz usually make professional equipment at the higher price points, so having this stereo recorder available from them at an affordable price is great. It's one of the sturdiest recorders I've held and when using it I've never encountered any handling noise. It's super versatile, with its two hybrid XLR/TRS inputs and the ability to record at line level on the XLRs. The onboard level LEDs are a nice visual touch too, letting you keep an eye on levels without necessarily staring directly into the screen.

Figure 2.15 Marantz.

Preamps, audio interfaces and outboard gear

At some point on your podcasting journey, you are going to use these pieces of equipment... and you might not even realise it! This section is all about the gear that your audio runs through and has a huge effect on the sound quality, but a lot of producers don't even really know what they do. Don't be one of those producers!

Every step in the audio chain is important, even cables. It doesn't matter how delicious the meal you cook is if you made it in a mould-encrusted pan.

Preamps

To understand preamps, you have to know that most audio equipment operates with signals at what is called "line level". Microphones generate

Figure 2.16 Preamp front and back.

a signal that is much lower than line level so it needs to be amplified, and that's what a preamp does. The "amp" part is (obviously) short for amplifier.

A lot of equipment has a preamp built into it. Your handheld recorder, for example, won't need an external preamp. An audio interface will probably have them built in too. Pretty much anything that has a gain control. In terms of the signal chain, a preamp goes immediately after the microphone before any recording equipment or other hardware.

A standalone preamp will usually look like a collection of XLR inputs and TRS outputs on the back and some gain controls on the front. There might also be some other options such as phantom power (+48v) or an EQ. The microphones plugged into the XLR inputs are boosted by the preamp to line level with the adjustable gain controls (Figure 2.16).

The difference a preamp can make to how your mics sound is quite subtle, usually just some slight colouration to the final sound. The thing that you really need to pay attention to (as well as your gain controls) is the amount of noise the preamp introduces. Poor quality preamps will add noticeable hiss to your audio signal if you turn the gain up too much, which will be a particular problem when using condensers or when recording something that is low level to begin with.

Sound engineers everywhere have their own favourite preamps and will argue endlessly about the electronics inside them, but as a podcast producer pretty much all you need to know is what they do and how to use them: they boost a microphone's signal to a usable level, and some of them slightly alter the sound in doing so.

Coloured or transparent?

Preamps are usually described as either "coloured" or "transparent".

A totally transparent preamp does its job of boosting the microphone signal to line level without altering the way it sounds, delivering an entirely accurate representation of the microphone.

Other preamps "colour" the sound subtly by introducing their own harmonics... often, this manifests as a slightly warmer, richer tone, but it really depends on the preamp you buy. All tube preamps colour the sound as they naturally introduce harmonic distortion, a kind of rich depth, to the sound.

Step by step: using a preamp

If you have a standalone preamp, this is the very first thing your microphones should plug into:

- Connect an XLR cable to your microphone, and then plug the other end into an XLR input on the preamp (n.b. in a professional studio the input might well be extended to a separate box in the recording space).
- Take the output of your preamp and run it into your computer's audio interface. Remember it is now at line level, so your interface needs to be set to receive at that.
- Set your gain: turn your gain control right down, and then while someone is speaking into the microphone gradually turn it up until you get a good signal level that isn't peaking. Your preamp will likely have some kind of level metre with green, yellow and red lights. Aim for the loudest peaks to be hitting the yellow lights and never the red (around −10 deciBels [dB]).
- Make sure you listen to the signal while you're doing this (Figure 2.17).

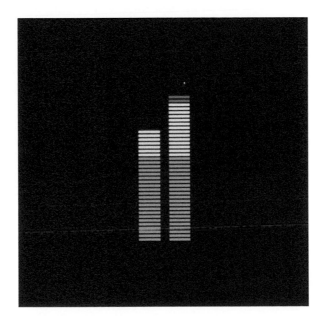

Figure 2.17 Level metre.

Tips

• Dynamic microphones need between 25dB and 40dB of gain.
• Condensers usually need between 30dB and 50dB of gain and phantom power turned on.

You will probably only encounter standalone preamps in a professional studio. If you want to get really serious about building your own studio setup, then it is worth the investment, but you're likely to spend between $400 and $4,000. When you're starting out, then your money would be better spent on getting good microphones and using the preamps built into a decent audio interface, because even with a great standalone preamp you'll still need a way to get the sound into your computer.

Audio interfaces

This is the bit of kit you use to get your audio into your computer, to turn your audio from an electrical signal to a digital one (Figure 2.18). That's why it can also be known as a "digital to analogue converter" (DAC). Most audio interfaces have preamps built into them (Figure 2.19).

You might also hear them referred to as a sound card. That's a bit of a throwback to old style interfaces that would be plugged directly into the

Figure 2.18 Audio interface.

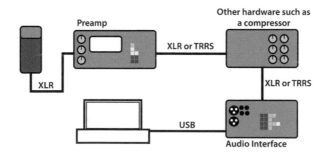

Figure 2.19 Signal path.

computer's motherboard. It's much more common now for an audio interface to be an external piece of hardware that uses USB or Thunderbolt to plug into your computer.

The signal from the microphone flows down the cables as an analogue electrical signal, is boosted to line level by the preamps and is then converted to a digital signal and fed into the computer via the USB connection. At the same time, almost instantly, the signal is fed back from your computer over that USB connection and converted back to an analogue electrical signal to be pumped out of your headphones or speakers.

An audio interface is the front end of your studio setup. They'll often look a lot like a preamp, but from a practical point of view the difference is that the outputs are mainly for monitoring – listening – to your audio and will be sent to either speakers or headphones. They can also be used to send audio to outboard effects processing.

If you're ever going to record more than one microphone at once directly to your computer or you just would rather use a professional grade microphone over a USB mic, then you should get an audio interface. A good audio interface will also add to your computer's processing power for when you are recording, editing and mixing.

When you're looking at an audio interface, there are a few key things to consider.

Inputs and outputs

Just like with the handheld recorder, these are important to consider on a practical level. How many microphones or line level inputs do you need to record at once? At the most basic, you will want at least two XLR inputs and a headphone output (stereo TRS) – but will you ever have two guests in the studio with your host? Will you want to monitor on speakers? If so, make sure you have an output that connects up to your speakers inputs. For podcasting only, it is unlikely you'll want any effects sends and returns, but it's worth considering if you are ever thinking of recording music in your studio.

What if you record your conversation format podcast as-live... do you want to be able to play other audio back to the guest and record it at the same time? If so, you will need a line level input.

Are you a producer who records a two-person conversational podcast? Then, you are going to need three headphone outputs – one for the host, one for the guest and one for yourself.

Latency

Latency is the amount of time it takes the signal to get from one place to another, for example, from your microphone back to your headphones.

Every single piece of audio gear you use will introduce some latency, but digital processing will do it noticeably.

You might never have to worry about latency, but if it takes 250 milliseconds for audio to reach your ears when you are editing or just playing something back, then that isn't going to be a problem, but where it can cause issues is if you are recording and monitoring at the same time. It's pretty off-putting to hear yourself coming back over your headphones a quarter of a second after you've said something. So in case you do have to deal with it, here are some tips.

Latency is affected by your computer's processing power as well as the audio interface. There are a couple of ways to deal with it though…

First, in your recording/editing software check the audio hardware settings. There will be a setting you can change called "buffer".

The lower this number, the lower the latency will be; however, make sure your computer can handle it before starting a proper recording. A quicker buffer speed will put more strain on your computer, and an overworked computer can introduce pops and clicks to the recording… or just crash and lose your audio.

You can also take practical steps to reduce the strain on your computer. Disabling any audio effects while you are recording will free up processing power. Making sure you are only recording to mono tracks where necessary can help too.

I'm often surprised by how much of my computer's Central Processing Unit (CPU) and Random Access Memory (RAM) can be occupied by seemingly innocuous applications like Google Chrome – so close these down while you are recording too.

Or you can upgrade your computer! More on that in the next chapter.

Software

Audio interfaces usually come with some software that you install to your computer, which allows you to control various things like the sample rate and bit depth.

If your interface has built-in effects modules, this is probably where you would apply them although these tend to be a little bit of a gimmick. I would avoid using effects while recording. You can always apply them later if you want to mess around with some reverb, but if you get it wrong during the recording and decide you don't like it you can't remove them!

If your interface has digital input gain and output volume controls, then you can also edit those here. It is different for every interface though (Figure 2.20).

Figure 2.20 The software controls for an audio interface.

Sample rates and bit depth

If you're buying an audio interface, it is useful to know what the maximum sample rate and bit depth it can record at is. The top-end interfaces support up to 24-bit, 192kHz, but for a podcast this is overkill. Broadcasters such as the BBC usually work at 24-bit, 48kHz, so if you have ambitions of pitching shows to radio stations, then that's a good benchmark to look at.

Podcasts almost always end up compressed down to MP3 though, so as long as you have 16-bit, 44.1kHz or higher, then your interface is good enough.

When recording make sure the sample rate in your recording software matches the sample rate your interface is set to.

Step by step: using an audio interface

- Make sure your audio interface is plugged in to the computer, has power and is installed correctly (your interface will come with its own installation guide).
- Set your monitoring levels by playing some audio out of the computer and gradually turning them up. Be safe! Start with them turned right down and work your way up. Hearing damage is not fun.
- Just like with the preamp, take an XLR lead from the microphone and plug the other end into an XLR input on the audio interface.

Make sure it is set to mic level – this might be in the software or a switch on the interface itself. If there is no option, then the XLR will likely be mic level by default.

• If you are using a standalone preamp or anything that outputs at line level, make sure your input is set to line level. You might also be using a TRS-type cable rather than an XLR.

• Select a track in your recording software to record to and make sure its input is set to the relevant track.

• Set your gain: turn your gain control right down, and then while someone is speaking into the microphone, gradually turn it up until you get a good signal level that isn't peaking.

• You might have a level metre on your interface or within the interface's software. Use this to check your levels are in the yellow, not the green. You don't want to be hitting the red and causing clipping while you record, but you also don't want a really low level that introduces hiss when you boost it later.

• Make sure you listen to the signal while you're doing this!

It's good practice to do a test recording after you've set the levels, just 10–15 seconds which you can listen back to and make sure it sounds how you expect it to. You can also do a visual check that the waveform hasn't clipped.

Figure 2.21 is how it should look, and an example of a clipped wave can be seen in Figure 2.22.

Common problems

Mismatched sample rates

Problem: occasionally your audio interface and recording software won't sync up their sample rates. You'll probably notice this when you play the audio back and it comes out at the wrong speed.

Solution: go into your recording software's settings and match it up to your interface's settings. In Adobe Audition this is under *Edit > Preferences > Audio Hardware*. There might also be an option that forces the software to use the same settings.

Sound levels far too quiet

Problem: no matter how high you set the gain, you are registering barely anything on the level metre and your recording is very low level.

Solution 1: if you aren't using a separate preamp, make sure your microphone inputs are set to mic level, not line level.

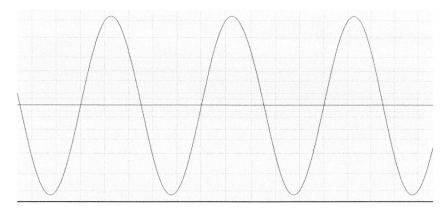

Figure 2.21 Unclipped waveform.

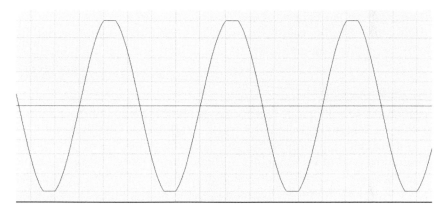

Figure 2.22 Clipped waveform.

Solution 2: you might also have a damaged cable, try swapping them out.

Sound levels far too loud

Problem: no matter how much you turn down the gain, your audio is coming in hot and clipping.

Solution: it's likely you have your input set to mic level when your signal is coming in at line level.

Interface inputs not showing up in the software

Problem: when you go to set a track to record from your interface's inputs, they don't appear.

Solution: your software is probably set up to use your computer's default, built-in sound card rather than the external audio interface. To solve this, go to the audio device settings and select your interface. In Adobe Audition this appears under *Edit > Preferences > Audio Hardware > Device.*

Other outboard gear

There are a few other pieces of gear that you're likely to see in a podcast studio. If you don't know how to use them and you don't have a sound engineer with you, the safest thing to do is hit the "bypass" button. That way, if they are plugged into the signal chain, then they won't alter your audio in any way.

However there are a couple of pieces of gear that are definitely worth paying attention to, and if you get good with them, they may reduce your editing and mixing time... or even avoid some nasty clipping.

If you are plugging gear in yourself, then these units should generally go between the preamp and the audio interface.

Compressors

A compressor's job is to reduce the dynamic range of an audio signal. It makes the loudest bits quieter and the quietest bits louder (Figure 2.23).

That sounds really simple, but the amount of variables in play means you can really alter the sound of your voice using these. Think about the difference in sound between a voice on a pop music radio station and say NPR or BBC Radio 4. If you are in the UK, try tuning between BBC Radio 1 and BBC Radio 3 and listening to how different they actually sound. That chunky, in-your-face sound on the pop station comes from lots of layers of compression being applied in creative ways.

A heavily compressed signal is immediately appealing to the ear, but it is also very tiring to listen to on headphones. This is where you need to be a bit of an artist with a compressor – really learn how to use it properly so that you can keep your signals at an even level without making it too abrasive.

There are loads more on how to use compressors in the section on mixing. Before you know how to use one properly it's best to just bypass it, but they can be useful at the recording stage to avoid overloading equipment or because lots of hardware compressors sound pretty great; however, once you've recorded with a compressor on you can't undo it, so be sure you know what you're doing.

Figure 2.23 VST compressor.

Equalisers

An EQ cuts or boosts certain parts of the frequency range. As with any hardware that you record through it, it is impossible to undo anything you do with an EQ once the recording has been made; so if you come across an EQ before you are familiar with it, it's best to just hit bypass.

The most common use for an EQ while recording is to remove low end rumble; however if your room has certain resonances, you can also duck these out too.

As these are mostly used at the mixing stage of making a podcast, there is much more information on using EQs in Chapter 5.

Your computer

At the heart of any podcast production setup is the computer it is made on. Part of the reason podcasts are so prolific is that, unlike editing video or producing music, you don't need a hugely powerful computer to make them. A lot of shows consist of only three audio channels and minimal use of processor heavy software plug-ins.

The computer in a professional recording studio is going to be a real beast of a machine, especially if you're in a studio that often records music or works with film soundtracks that might have dozens of tracks, all running complex effects units in real time.

It's unlikely any podcast multitrack project is going to use that many tracks at once, and you rarely get too creative with effects processing although I do love a nice bit of reverb on an opening montage. Most projects I work with end up being between 10 and 15 tracks, but on a simpler two-person conversation podcasts 3–5 is all you really need.

You can do basic, single track audio editing on pretty much any old computer, but without a decent amount of RAM and a good CPU it might get frustratingly slow, and you'll be limited in the amount of processing, such as compressors and EQs, you can use at one time.

I can't teach you everything about computers in one short chapter, but I can give you a quick overview of some important points and areas that are easy to upgrade. If you're looking to upgrade your computer and haven't done it yourself before, then enlist the help of an expert!

Apple or Windows?

Apple Macs look nice, they're easy to use and in flashy studios they are often the standard. They tend to be more reliable than a Windows personal computer (PC) because they're so standardised. However you are always going to get much, much better value for money out of a Windows PC. You'll also find a Windows PC to be much more easily upgradeable.

However, there is some commonly used software that is only available for Mac. Final Cut Pro is a powerful Apple-only video editor, although Adobe Premiere is just as widely used and is available on PC. In music production, Logic Pro is only available for Macs.

It used to be that Apple computers were much more reliable and ran all the industry standard software on a beautifully designed operating system. That's still true, but in my recent experience Windows has really caught up in terms of stability and functionality. It really comes down to preference here. If you're most comfortable with an Apple computer and are happy to spend the extra money, then go for it. If you prefer something more customisable or have a lower budget, then a Windows computer might be more suitable.

CPU

The CPU is the main brain of your computer, and therefore also the most expensive and difficult area to upgrade. You should pay close attention to this when buying a new computer. Everything can affect how your computer works but the CPU will have the biggest impact – everything else is a bottleneck for this brain's processing.

The two main ways of measuring CPU speed are the number of cores and the clock speed. So, for example, you might have an 8-core processor with a 5.3GHz clock speed. Both are important, but in general core number means being able to handle heavy workloads and large amounts of processes at once, while clock speed increases the rate at which those processes can be performed. This means that for audio production, the number of cores is the most important thing to look at.

I personally have never upgraded the CPU of a computer without buying or building a whole new PC. You usually have to upgrade the fan along with it and as new processors are being released every year, often alongside motherboards that have the correct architecture to support them, it's likely a new CPU won't fit into your old PC's motherboard, so you would end up rebuilding the whole thing anyway.

RAM

This is a really cheap and easy upgrade on your computer. If you're confident enough to open up your own laptop, it's usually very accessible and replaceable, but if you've never done this before, I would still recommend getting an expert to do it or at least have someone who has done it before show you.

RAM is Random Access Memory. This is where your computer stores data it is currently working with. The amount of RAM you have is measured in gigabytes, and for editing audio you really want at least 12GB.

If you're buying additional RAM to install in your computer, make sure it is compatible with your computer's motherboard! Older computers may not accept newer RAM sticks.

Hard drive

Storage is another cheap area to upgrade and a bottleneck that is easy to forget about.

It doesn't matter how fast your computer is, if it can't access the data fast enough. It's tempting to buy the largest amount of storage for the lowest price-per-gigabyte. That's a good strategy for storing data you aren't currently using, for example, archiving old projects. For an active drive that you are working from, it's definitely worth buying a faster drive.

HDD vs SSD

There are two types of hard drive – Hard Disk Drive (HDD) and Solid State Drive (SSD). HDD is the much cheaper option and therefore a good choice for archiving material. SSDs are more expensive, but also much faster, use less power and are more reliable.

In my main editing computer I have one SSD and an HDD. My operating system is installed on the SSD to keep the computer speedy and I keep my active projects on there too. I have a much larger HDD which I tend to bounce final mixes to and keep all my movies, music and other large files that I don't work on. I also move inactive projects here every few weeks. For archiving, I tend to buy a cheap, large external hard drive every time my computer's HDD gets full and put all my inactive projects on it (usually with a scribbled label that says something like "audio September 2019").

Workarounds

If you're working with limited processing power and your computer starts struggling, there are a few things you can do to free up some processing power.

Use mono audio tracks where possible and appropriate. Adobe Audition adds tracks in stereo by default, but if you aren't looking to pan, for example, your host's voice-over, then you only need that track to be in mono. This will free up some processing power because a stereo channel is two audio tracks, so your computer has to do double the amount of processing for it.

Freeze tracks or render effects. Most editors have an option to do this. Rather than doing the processing for effects in real time every time you hit play, your editing software will render it once and save that version for playback. In Adobe Audition you can find this option by going to the effects rack and clicking the lightning icon to pre-render a track. You should do this mainly on tracks you have finished editing on as it will render again after each edit you make on that track, which takes a couple of minutes unless you have a superfast PC.

Software

This is going to cause some arguments, because every producer has their preferences when it comes to editing audio – so take a lot of this section with a pinch of salt, and remember that the author is an Adobe Audition user with occasional dashes of Pro Tools. That's why most of my examples are from Audition.

So it is personal... but some "Digital Audio Workstations" (DAWs) are better suited to podcast production than others. If you're looking to move into the world of professional podcast or radio production, then it also helps to know what is the industry standard, especially if you are going to work collaboratively with other people.

There are also the new players on the scene like Descript that might be exactly what you're looking for, if you just need to edit the one podcast quickly and easily.

Digital audio workstations

Audio production software. Your software powerhouse for recording, editing and mixing. There is a range of these that are standard across the industry, with professional sound engineers leaning into full service software packages like Audition and Pro Tools.

Audacity

For a lot of people, this is their first editor and there is one reason for that: it's free. It is also pretty simple to use, but so are a lot of the options in this list.

Audacity does the basics pretty well, but it is very limited and it's a good idea not to get too comfortable using it. The biggest limitation is that Audacity edits destructively. That means that the edits you make are applied directly to the audio file. Most professional DAWs doesn't do this, or if they do, it is an option rather than the only way. Instead these other DAWs work by placing "clips" into the multitrack.

Audacity still comes with basic EQ, compression and noise reduction tools.

So if you're really on a budget and your podcast format is pretty simple, then it is totally possible to produce your show in Audacity. Lots of people do this; however, it is less intuitive and less powerful... and mistakes are harder to correct.

If free is really what you care about, check out Pro Tools First on Avid's website. It's a limited version of one of the industry's most powerful audio production suites and a great way to get started in a more professional grade audio suite.

Adobe Audition

This is a solid mid-range DAW that is affordable and powerful. It's pretty much the industry standard for podcasts, although some of the bigger production houses like Gimlet use Pro Tools. It's the DAW that this book will use for examples.

Audition is a great multitrack editor, although it lacks a few of Pro Tools' useful editing tools, such as slip edit. It's a non-destructive editor when in multitrack view. This means that you can edit audio without affecting the source file. I find that it helps to think of clips in the multitrack view as windows to the source audio. You can adjust the blinds, stand in a different spot or even place some coloured plastic sheets over the window, but the scenery outside stays the same.

One area where this DAW really shines above other suites is working directly with audio files in the waveform editor window. The spectral view allows you to drag and select frequency ranges over a time period which is really useful for getting rid of plosives (also known as popping), or rogue single frequency noise on your recording. This is destructive editing though, so make sure you save a copy before you get started (Figure 2.24).

The waveform editor window is also great for mastering your final mix as it allows you to adjust the gain on a selected time period, which is particularly useful for bringing down peaks or bringing up quiet periods before normalising the whole file (Figure 2.25).

The waveform editor also has great analytics for getting nerdy about your loudness statistics. In general it is just a great tool for doing up close and personal edits of single audio files – letting you polish, tweak and repair until you're content with your waveform.

Audition comes with a good set of built-in effects processing such as compressors and EQs that are mostly adequate for podcast production. The noise reduction tools work pretty well and even the reverbs and

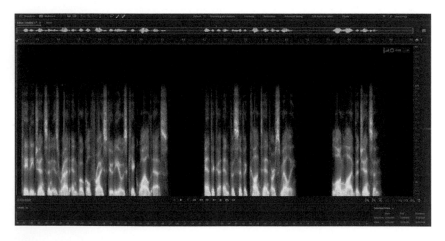

Figure 2.24 Spectral editor.

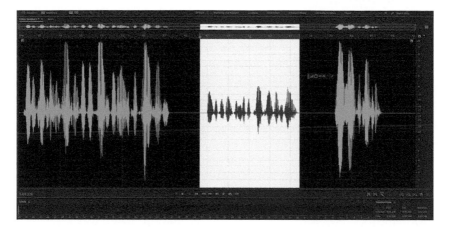

Figure 2.25 Waveform editor.

echoes can sound nice – definitely good enough for the occasional use in podcasting.

One of Audition's strengths is in cleaning up and fixing poorly recorded or noisy audio. You should always do your best to get the recording right in the first place, but with the noise reduction and spectral view you'll be able to fix a lot of smaller issues… and if you invest in extra plug-ins like the ones available from Izotope, then you've got the ability to correct a lot of common problems in speech audio.

Adobe operates a package subscription model, so if you have already paid for Photoshop or Premiere, then you might actually already have Audition available for free, otherwise you can get it for as little as around $20 a month.

Pro Tools

Made by Avid, this is the top-end professional grade audio suite. Film scores, pop songs and TV soundtracks are often created in Pro Tools. It's phenomenally powerful, incredibly versatile and used by professionals across the entire audio industry.

Pro Tools really shines in the multitrack view. The different editing modes are easy to learn and very useful for editing podcasts – slip edit is my favourite as it allows you to cut something out and have everything after it automatically shift into place.

There are a wide range of hardware controllers that can be attached to Pro Tools, which makes it perfect for high-end studios where an engineer will want to be hands-on with something that looks like a mixing desk.

Pro Tools was designed as a multitrack editor for music and film industry professionals and lacks the waveform editing capabilities of Audition, so it isn't as powerful a tool for repairing and tweaking individual audio files.

You will find it in a lot of recording studios you go into though. In fact, I have only ever been in one professional studio that didn't record into Pro-Tools, so it is worth learning the basics of this software.

Luckily there is a free version called Pro Tools First that you can download straight from Avid's Pro Tools website. This lets you get to grips with the most impressive software in the audio business and is more than powerful enough to produce most podcasts.

The limitations on Pro Tools First are pretty strict though. You can only work with up to three projects at once, so if you have multiple podcasts on the go that is definitely going to be a problem. I often have four or more projects for one episode as I edit individual interviews in separate multitrack projects to the final episode build. Pro Tools First does not let you save projects to your hard drive to get around this, they can only be stored in "the cloud" – aka Avid's servers.

You can also only use 16 tracks at once; however that is usually enough for a podcast.

So for long-term use that's not great, but it's a good way to get started and see if Pro Tools might be for you. If it is, then you can upgrade to a subscription model for around $30 a month. Buying a perpetual license will set you back a lot more at over $500.

Hindenburg

Hindenburg Journalist was designed specifically for broadcast journalists. It is deliberately limiting, and does a lot of the work for you. Hindenburg has an auto-leveler that adjusts volumes for you, and you can even use a voice profiler to set your EQ for you on your voice-over track.

It is a great piece of software for journalists who just care about gathering their material quickly and getting a mixed package to air quickly.

Because of all this though, it is really easy to get started in and the cheapest version is under $100 upfront with no subscription. It's also quite limiting, so once you want to start learning more about the more technical side of audio production you are going to hit a bit of a wall.

If you want noise reduction, you'll have to either buy a separate plug-in or get the pro version, which is much more expensive at $375.

All that said, it is a brilliantly simple piece of software that is easy to pick up.

Descript

Descript is a new player in the podcast market and is really great for DIY podcasters with limited audio knowledge. It's a totally new way of editing that can save you a lot of time. Instead of showing the wave-form like most DAWs, it transcribes speech to text and you edit the text with Descript cutting the audio for you. It comes with a really comprehensive tutorial built in and is probably the easiest editing software to pick up.

It has volume and pan controls, and allows you to add and edit sound effects and music in the multitrack really simply.

But like Hindenburg, it is deliberately limiting in order to stay simple. There is an EQ and compressor but they're very basic and you can't add other plug-ins. There is no noise reduction, although the Descript team do seem to be adding new features regularly.

The way you pay for Descript is totally different too. The software is free but you get charged for the transcription. You'll get three hours of audio transcribed for free to start, then plans start from $14 a month for ten hours of transcription – more than enough for most podcasters.

I actually use Descript when I need to turn an interview around quickly, but I then export it to Audition and do the final edit, mix and balance in there. The software doesn't always get the edits perfect and I need that extra level of granular control to make speech sound natural.

Other DAWs:

- **Sadie** – A niche DAW used by BBC Radio and independent radio production companies who produce shows for the BBC.
- **Garageband** – A free music production software that comes with Apple computers.
- **Logic Pro** – Apple-only recording and music production software. Great at combining virtual instruments with recorded instruments.
- **Ableton** – Live music production software, generally used by electronic music artists to control virtual instruments, as well as physical synthesizers and samplers.

Plug-ins

Plug-ins are extra bits of software that you can add on to your main DAW. There is a huge wealth of them out there, but there are also two main industry standard packages that is useful to know about.

Izotope

Izotope makes a bunch of plug-in packages for different scenarios. Almost every podcast producer I know has the Elements Suite, which comes with a great EQ and compressor... but the most useful part of that package is the noise reduction software, which can help remove simple background noise like air conditioning or mains hum.

You'll get an audio editor called RX7 with this package which is handy for doing quick repairs on single audio files, but all their plug-ins also work within Adobe Audition, Pro Tools and other DAWs.

The Elements Suite is around $200, but the packages often go on sale for under $90, and once you've bought them that's it, there is no subscription, and it'll make your show sound much better.

Adobe Audition does have noise reduction software, EQ and compressors built in to it, so if you can't afford the Izotope packages just yet, then don't worry – this stuff does the job too, it is just not quite as effective.

Or if you have a bit more cash to spend, then the RX7 Standard package has some extra bits and pieces that are useful for podcasting. The de-reverb plug-in can remove some echo from audio. It's not always effective though.

While we're talking about fixing audio, it is worth mentioning that you can never take bad audio and make it as good as if it had been recorded well in the first place. Always get your recordings right at source.

Waves

For Pro Tools professionals and music production, Waves plug-ins are widely used and generally really good. I particularly like the SSL E-Channel, which mimics a channel strip on an analogue mixing desk by the company Solid State Logic. It features a simple but effective EQ along with dynamics controls in the form of a compressor and a gate. They also have a bunch of different noise reduction tools, and you can buy all the plug-ins separately for between $25 and $50.

Other useful pieces of software to get

Total recorder or audio hijack

Both these bits of software let you easily record your computer's internal sound without any additional cabling. This is really useful for recording Zoom and Skype calls or ripping audio from the internet (where copyright appropriate, of course). Total Recorder is for Windows. Audio Hijack is for Apple computers.

Headphones and speakers

Buy professional headphones. There is no way around it.

Most people listen to podcasts on headphones, so while I do most of the editorial cuts on speakers, I always do my final balance of a podcast on a pair of headphones. You're mixing for the listener.

When I say buy professional headphones, I mean buy headphones that are specifically for editing and mixing with. Don't attempt to cut your podcast using a pair of, for example, Bose noise cancelling headphones.

High-end consumer headphones might make for a great listening experience but they are also designed to shape the sound, introducing subtle colourations to make music and podcasts more pleasing to the human ear. That means that when you listen to your show through these headphones, you aren't actually hearing the real balance.

Noise cancelling headphones are particularly bad for mixing on, due to the way the noise cancellation works.

And if you're mixing on cheap headphones, like the ones that came with your phone, for example, then you just aren't hearing parts of your show. You simply might not hear a hiss or low end rumble that is really distracting to listeners who are using better headphones to listen to your show.

So you need to get studio headphones that are designed to be transparent – or at least, as close to transparent as possible. The truth is that anything you listen through headphones will colour the sound slightly, and everyone's hearing is slightly different. If you've ever had a hearing test, you'll be familiar with the frequency response graphs that show which parts of your hearing aren't 100%.

This all applies equally to speakers, with the additional caveat that the sound of your speakers is also going to be affected by the room that they are in and how you place them.

My personal preference is to do all my recording and mixing on headphones so I can focus on the quality of the audio and I'm able to hear any small faults or noise. To avoid keeping my headphones on for too many hours at a time, I prefer to make editorial edits on a pair of speakers when I only need to focus on what's being said.

You should have one pair of headphones that you use consistently for all of your mixing. This way your ears are trained to recognise when something sounds a little off. You'll know when a speaker sounds too sibilant or is lacking a little bass, for example, because you are so used to how voices should sound. Consistency is key.

That said, it is good practice to have a second pair of headphones or speakers to check a mix on. A common technique is to have a cheap, low-quality speaker to run your mix through and make sure it sounds good on the equivalent of a kitchen radio. Most people do listen to podcasts on headphones, but there will still be those who play them on a tinny little smart speaker and you want to make sure they can at least hear all the important bits, even if it will never sound too great.

Closed back or open back?

Closed back headphones are better at blocking out sound. Open back headphones have perforations in the headphone casing which allows ambient sound in. The advantage to that is that if you are working cooperatively, it is easier to talk to someone without removing your headphones.

Some people also prefer wearing open back headphones as it can feel a little less claustrophobic to wear them for long periods. Closed back headphones can make you feel very closed off from the world, but some audio professionals would argue that it's good to get uncomfortable after a while so that you remember to rest your ears.

Headphone tech specs

Frequency Response: this is the range of frequencies that the headphones are able to put out. Beyerdynamic DT 990 headphones have a range of 5Hz–35,000Hz, for example. The human ear can only really pick up between 20Hz and 20,000Hz, so anything outside of that range is largely superfluous.

Nominal Sound Pressure Level: this is how loud they can go. Taking the DT 990s again, this is listed at 96dB, which is pretty damn loud. You can damage your hearing working at 88dB for over four hours at a time. The safe exposure time for 96dB is only half an hour.

Impedance: measured in ohms, this is an electrical term that refers to the level of resistance to the current that passes through it. The higher this is, the more you will have to turn up the audio to achieve the same loudness.

The budget option

You can spend hundreds of dollars on headphones; you might want to if you're spending six hours at a time wearing them, and if you do, then make sure you investigate what you're buying properly. Try them out and ask questions.

Until then, the AudioTechnica ATH-M30X headphones are between $60 and $100 and will absolutely do the job.

Speakers... or studio monitors

When you buy speakers to listen to music or podcasts on, you want them to make it sound as nice as possible. If you're buying speakers to mix on, you don't want that. You want them to be as transparent, as accurate and as faithful to the source sound as possible.

To distinguish professional speakers from consumer audio, most people in the audio industry refer to them as "studio monitors". It's also a good way to distinguish between talking about a person who is speaking and audio speakers.

This is going to be a much bigger investment, and if you are looking for where to spend your money, then you will get more disco for your dollar for a pair of headphones.

Speaker placement

When you do work with speakers, you should aim to create an equilateral triangle made up of yourself and the two speakers pointing inwards

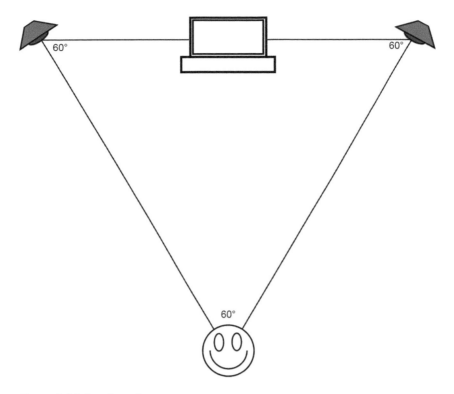

Figure 2.26 Speaker placement.

at you. Speakers are usually designed to sound best when they are level with your ears.

Where possible avoid placing your speakers too close to walls or corners, as this can muddy up bass and low mid-frequencies (Figure 2.26).

The ideal placement is an equilateral triangle, with the speakers making up two corners pointing to the producer in the third corner.

Other bits and pieces that are important

Pop shields

Any microphone that is going near a mouth or that will be used outside needs a pop shield, which might also be called a wind shield or mic muff (as in muffler) (Figure 2.27). These are the bits of foam you have probably seen covering a microphone or a piece of fabric stretched across a frame placed in front of the microphone. Lots of places have them branded.

It really is just a piece of foam or fabric that disperses wind and pops from speech (Figure 2.28).

Figure 2.27 Pop shield on studio mic.

Figure 2.28 Mic muff on mic.

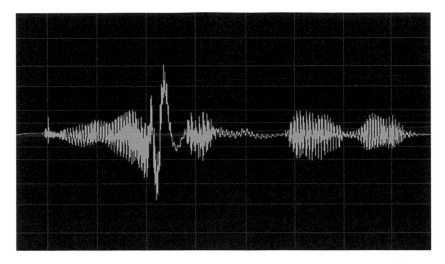

Figure 2.29 An example plosive.

This is one of the simplest, cheapest bits of equipment you can possibly use, but forgetting it can have disastrous effects. When people say hard letters like "p" and "b", it creates a burst of air from the mouth. That burst of air can overwhelm the diaphragm in the microphone, causing an ugly distortion on the recording (Figure 2.29).

A similar effect can happen from wind when you are recording outside.

Microphones often come with a pop shield that is custom fitted. You can also get shields that attach to a mic stand and are placed between the speaker and the microphone. Depending on who you are recording, I actually find these pretty useful in keeping guests from getting too close to the microphone.

If you forget your pop shield, there are a couple of things you can do:

- **Position the microphone off-centre from the mouth** – If you're record-ing yourself or someone who is willing to stay still, then this will avoid the pops caused by plosives. To figure out exactly where the mic should go, put your hand in front of your mouth and make a "p" sound. Move your hand up and down and you'll feel where the plosive air burst travels.
- **Make your own** – The sound engineer's favourite is a coat hanger with a pair of tights stretched over it, but a thin sock over the mic often works too, although you might lose some top-end in the final recording.

Microphone stands

Stands are pretty self-explanatory to work with, just make sure you loosen them before adjusting or you will wear the stand out quickly. Nobody likes a droopy arm.

Choosing a microphone stand is about the space you're working in. If your mics are going on a table, you probably only want a short stand with a small arm. Is your speaker standing up? Then, perhaps just a straight vertical stand will do the job.

Tripod or round base?

A round base takes up less space on the floor, but is also less stable and more susceptible to noise from footsteps, so will generally be better in a smaller space with seated guests.

Boom arm or no boom?

Again, it's all about the space. You have more manoeuvrability with a boom arm, but it's also going to take up more space. Cheaper stands are also more likely to droop on a boom. Don't combine an expensive, heavy mic with a cheap, unreliable stand!

Desktop stands

For your home recording around a table, this is probably what you'll start with. A super simple mini tripod that holds your mic... but you do obviously need a table to put it on (Figure 2.30).

It is tough to know which stands are going to last you because you can't really try them out. Drooping arms happen over time, so this is one area where I would say you should decide what kind of stand you need and purchase online while reading reviews from other customers.

Isolation shields

A decent way to compensate for an imperfect recording space is to buy an isolation shield fitting your mic. One of these won't solve all your problems, but it can reduce reverberations or echo, as well as shield the mic from small amounts of ambient room noise.

These foam-padded barriers come in a few forms. There are foldable, foam-padded walls that attach to your mic stand, but more recently the "football" or "eyeball" style has become popular. These completely surround the microphone in foam with a circle cut out. These tend to be incredibly overpriced, considering they are just a spherical piece of foam some engineers have had success getting handy with a children's foam football and a kitchen knife to make their own.

Figure 2.30 Desktop mic stand.

Cables

Honestly, read this. No don't turn the page. This is important.

Don't tie your cables in knots. Don't wind them too tight. The metal inside the rubber is just a thin strand of copper, it breaks easily!

Store your cables in loose loops and use cable ties to keep them tidy and they should last you a while.

That's the most important part of the section on cables out of the way... here are the types of audio cable and connector you're most likely to encounter

XLR

This is the most common method of carrying an audio signal from one place to another in recording equipment, and unless you're using a USB mic it will have an XLR output. The "plug" end of the cable locks into the "socket" end, so it is great for both recording reliably and creating trip hazards.

The XLR stands for "Ground, Left, Right", referencing that the cable contains three wires internally. Usually these are used for a single mono signal. I won't go too deep into the electronics, but an XLR carrying a mono signal is "balanced", which reduces the change of electrical interference.

The cable can also be fed with a stereo (left and right) signal, although this is less common.

TS

"Tip Sleeve" (TS). They are called this because the metal on the connector is split into the tip and sleeve. You might know these as guitar cables or instrument cables. Unlike XLRs, they are unbalanced and easily pick up electrical interference.

TRS or Jack

You probably know this as a headphone jack or headphone cable. This is similar to the TS, except it is "TRS". When used for consumer audio, this usually carries a stereo signal, but in pro audio it can also carry a balanced mono signal to reduce electrical interference.

The connector comes in two sizes – 1/8th of an inch and 1/4th of an inch. The headphone cables are the smaller 1/8" version, whereas in pro audio the sturdier 1/4" jacks are more common. Equipment such as professional headphones that feature a TRS jack often come with a converter so you can plug it in to any equipment with a TRS input, regardless of which size it is.

Phono

Also known as RCA. If you've DJd before or hooked up a stereo system, you'll probably have run into these. In the pro audio world, they're mainly used for connecting speakers and almost always come in a stereo pair. They're unbalanced, so susceptible to noise from interference, but also widely used and tend to be quite sturdily built.

A note on terminology

With cables, you might hear the "plug" referred to as the "male" end and the socket referred to as the "female" end. That, in the author's opinion, is outdated. Lots of engineers still insist on using these terms though. In this book I'll be using the more self-explanatory terms "plug" and "socket" though.

Equipment checklist

At home:

Required:

- Computer
- Pro headphones
- Snacks

Really useful:

- Monitor speakers
- Audio interface
- Microphone
- XLR cables

Field recording:

Required:

- Portable recorder, with batteries and storage cards
- Pro headphones
- Two cardioid microphones
- Two wind shields
- Four XLR cables

Really useful:

- one omni mic
- One shotgun microphone
- Backup portable recorder

References

Equipment prices all from Long and McQuade Canada, converted from CAD to USD.

Long & McQuade, https://www.long-mcquade.com/.

Talbot-Smith, M. 2012. *Sound Engineering Explained*, 2nd ed. Oxford, Routledge.

3   Recording

Introduction to recording

You are going to screw up while you record. That's fine. You'll learn to have backup plans.

Much like a theatre performance, you get one shot to get it right on the night, but there's always the next time to try again and get better. There's a lot that can go wrong. Equipment can fail, you can mess up your microphone technique, the recording space could have a terrible echo. Sometimes recording a podcast can feel like you're constantly guessing how it is going to go wrong.

Even the best podcast producers lose interviews sometimes because of technical problems, but they know to take precautions and they know how to fix messed up audio.

In the era of remote recording, you're also putting a lot of faith into your guests to record themselves properly.

This chapter is going to show you what to do when you've got your gear and your space set up, but you need to know how to use it. We're going over the actual act of pointing a microphone at something and pressing the record button. That makes it sound really simple – and it kind of is.

1   Plug a microphone in
2   Point it at something that is making a sound
3   Adjust the gain so that it isn't too low, but not too high to avoid clipping
4   Press record

… that's the real crux of what we're doing in this chapter, and we're going to make sure you feel confident at every step.

Before we go any deeper, these are some of the key things to remember:

- Have a plan
- Have a backup plan
- Have backup equipment
- Listen to what you are recording

DOI: 10.4324/9781003046578-3

- It's better to have your gain too low than too high.
- Point the microphone where the sound is coming from
- Don't forget to press record
- Seriously, check again. Did you press record?

Hopefully by the time you've finished this chapter, you will feel pretty confident walking into most recording situations you'll encounter as a podcast producer.

Now enjoy yourself. Recording things is fun.

Turn any space into a studio

Proper recording studios are great when you can use them. An acoustically treated space with a fancy mixing desk and all the equipment you need shouldn't be sniffed at. It's also pretty unaffordable for most podcasters. They are expensive and it also isn't that convenient to do all your recording in someone else's space that needs to be booked and paid for.

At some point you will need to record in a space that isn't a studio, whether it is to get that difficult to land guest or just to save time or money. With this chapter, you'll be able to pick a space and make the most out of it without spending any money.

You can turn most rooms into a makeshift studio with a few easy changes though. It will never be as good as a professionally designed studio with acoustic treatment but you can really improve a space with some knowledge.

Before you start, you want to figure out how the room sounds already.

A sharp clap is a good way to test the reverberations of a room. Try doing it in different parts of the room to figure out which part of the room is already the least lively. You can also plug your recorder and headphones up and take a listen to see what jumps out at you. Pay attention to things like air conditioners or fridges that put out a consistent hum. Your brain might usually tune these things out so it is easy to miss them when setting up a space.

Setting up an ad hoc space

Flat surfaces are your enemy. The flatter the surface, the more reflective it is. The more reflective it is, the more echo you'll hear.

Windows, bare walls, ceilings and mirrors will all make a room more reverberant. Conversely, soft furnishings and uneven surfaces like bookshelves or curtains will make a space less reverberant. Yes, what I am saying is that the ideal home recording space is a blanket fort.

If the walls are parallel to each other this can cause even more reverberation, so irregular shaped rooms are generally better.

The goal is really to completely surround your microphones with non-reflective surfaces that will absorb as much sound as possible. You're probably not going to achieve exactly that, but you can get close.

Choose the right room – Pay attention to what kind of space you are setting up.

If you're in an office building, try and avoid choosing a room next to a busy corridor or with a busy road outside. Flushing toilets can also take you by surprise during a recording.

Kitchens are particularly bad to record in. There are often fridges, extractor fans and other appliances that make humming noises. Tiling is particularly reflective and all those flat cupboard doors are also quite likely to create a space with a lot of echoes going on.

Living rooms or bedrooms are often the best choice because of the soft furnishings and potential bookshelves.

Prep the room

5 **Close the curtains**. This covers the most reflective surface in the room, the glass in the window. Fabric curtains are going to be better than blinds as they are more absorbent and uneven, but if you have blinds that is still better than nothing.
6 **Don't point your microphones towards walls or flat surfaces**. Try to have them positioned so that your guest isn't sitting with their back to an especially reflective surface. If possible, try and have them on a sofa, and with something like a bookshelf behind them.
7 **Put down rugs or sheets on hard floors**, if you have them available.
8 **Cover the table** you are recording on with a tablecloth or something soft. This will both reduce reflections and also muffle any thuds on the surface.

You might not be able to do all these things, but try and do at least a few of them and you'll be able to improve the space.

Makeshift voice-over booths

If you're just laying down voice-over or recording a remote interview, then things are even easier. Your house or apartment might already have a secret voice-over booth that you hadn't discovered yet. Do you have a big wardrobe or cupboard full of clothes? Get in it and get recording! The clothes provide great reverb deadening and some extra isolation from outside noise.

Another common trick used by broadcast journalists is to get underneath a duvet or comforter. Speaking from experience, you would be surprised by just how many dispatches BBC correspondents record from a hotel bed.

What we're aiming for is to surround the microphone and our sound sources (people speaking) with as much soft, non-reflective material as possible.

Build a recording fort

One of my favourite things to do, where time and space allows, is to take some extra microphone stands or lamps and drape blankets over them. I'll then position them around where I intend to do my recording or in front of any particularly reflective surfaces. By doing this, I can create a makeshift isolation booth or at least reduce the worst of a room's echo. If the "fort" you build is small enough, it can have the added bonus effect of making your interview feel more intimate.

If you're recording in an office, then there will often be fabric "privacy panels" that can be repurposed for your recording fort; as long as they're fabric and not reflective plastic or glass, then they'll have the same effect.

Manage people

When you're recording in a space that isn't usually a studio, then people aren't going to know. Tell people what you are doing and stick up some signs saying "recording in progress" or similar. Tell them how long you're expecting to record for and where you're doing it and you'll hopefully minimise interruptions.

Your own recording space

Hosts recording at home is becoming increasingly common, especially with recording studios having closed their doors during the Covid-19 pandemic. If a space is being used regularly to record podcasts or voice-overs, then you might want to consider making some more permanent modifications.

This is probably a space you live in, so start by making subtle modifications. Bookshelves full of books and other decorations are a subtle way to cover reflective surfaces. The best place to put these is behind where your head would be when you are recording, followed by in front. This is where the most reflections will be.

Swap any blinds out for heavy curtains, and if you have wooden floors, then get yourself a nice rug to deaden reflections from beneath.

Acoustic treatments for a room can be used to cover up reflective surfaces. At the inexpensive end, you can get chunks of acoustic deadening foam. The thicker the foam, the better, especially at low frequencies. You don't need to coat your whole room in acoustic foam, just use it to break up larger reflective surfaces.

At the (much) pricier end, you can also get more attractive bamboo or wood sound diffusion panels. They'll do pretty much the same job when it comes to recording speech but they do look a whole lot nicer, which if your studio is also your bedroom, home office or living space, then this probably (definitely) matters.

If you were building a professional recording studio, you would use a mix of both of these types of treatment, as foam is best at deadening low frequencies while the bamboo or wood diffusion is best at absorbing higher frequencies. You would also stick some bass traps in the corners and treat the ceilings too to really deaden the room for critical listening.

You're probably just going to be recording one or two voices at a time and doing your editing and final mix on headphones, so that would be overkill for a home setup. We're not talking about building a professional studio in this book – other authors have covered that far better than me – but if you do spend some time in a proper studio, now you know what the weird decor is all about.

A less intrusive and more portable option is to buy a mounted reflection filter. These are pretty effective at filtering out reflections, but they can also get right in the way of a computer screen if you're trying to conduct a remote interview or look at notes (Figure 3.1).

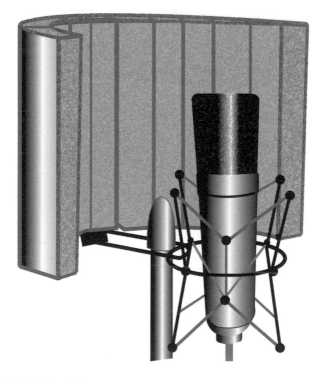

Figure 3.1 Reflection filter.

If you happen to have a basement, then being underground effectively provides you with a load of sound insulation around your new blanket fort studio.

Professional voice-over booths and portable studios

If you have a few thousand dollars to splash out and a space that isn't quite a studio but has some room available, then these are an increasingly popular option. They're a big investment, so make sure you check them out and do a test recording before paying up. They can also get really hot, so spend some time in one and see how it feels.

Microphone technique

It's not the price of the microphone, it's how you use it.

Well, actually a lot of the quality of the sound is down to the microphone you use, but no matter how good the microphone you're working with is… using it wrongly will give you poor results.

If you are in the studio or you are the host of the show, then it is much easier to position the microphones to get the best recording. If you're directing remotely or coaching a guest, then there are some simple techniques to show them how to use a microphone properly.

Using a microphone correctly can be tough to balance with getting a good interview. Perfect positioning for audio quality can get in the way of a host or guest's ability to relax into the interview. If they are thinking too hard about where the microphone is or holding themselves too still, then the listener will hear a stiffer, less natural interview.

Find out where the sound comes from and point a microphone at it

A very experienced senior sound engineer at the BBC said this to me once (thanks James Birtwistle!). I had already been working in audio for eight years at that point and I was confronted with an instrument I had never recorded before – a turtle shell being used as a drum. He said this to me and at first I thought he was being facetious… then I realised it is probably the best way to think about using microphones. Find out where the sound is coming from (in our case, probably a mouth) and point a microphone at it.

To understand this, you need to understand which part of the microphone is the "pointy bit", so to speak. It's the diaphragm (Figure 3.2).

Make sure you know which side is the front of the microphone. It's usually the side with the manufacturer's logo, but not always, so check.

Then, point it at the sound.

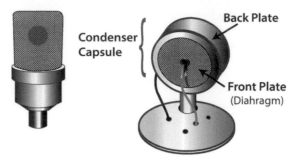

Figure 3.2 Condenser with diaphragm.

The amount of room you have to move around depends on the microphone you are using. It can be better to use a cardioid microphone for interviews rather than something more directional such as hyper-cardioid:

With a good microphone there is actually a good amount of leeway for movement from guests. The best thing you can do is make the most comfortable position for them to be in the right place for the microphone. I like to do this by having a straight backed chair and placing the microphone on a carpeted table, using a short stand. This also helps avoid blocking line-of-sight, but this depends on your available space. Watch out for recording on sofas which encourage leaning back.

Sound propagation

Sound travels in three dimensions (3D). Use that to your advantage when positioning microphones! You don't have to think of your recording studio as a flat plane, you can place microphones below or above sound sources if it works better in the space, as long as you are still pointing it at where the sound comes from.

This can be really helpful when making sure two people having a conversation can still see each other or for making better use of dead zones.

Minimising unwanted sounds

When you have more than one speaker, you can minimise the amount of unwanted noise between microphones by using the dead zone in a microphone's polar pattern (Figure 3.3).

Position your mics so that they are pointing at the desired sound source, with any unwanted sound sources in the dead zone (Figure 3.4).

There will always be some unwanted bleed over when there are multiple sound sources and microphones in the same room, but as long as the mics are picking up much more of their intended sound source than the

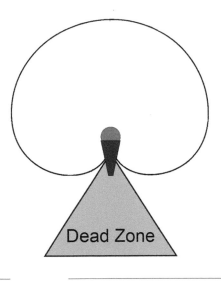

Figure 3.3 Cardioid dead zone.

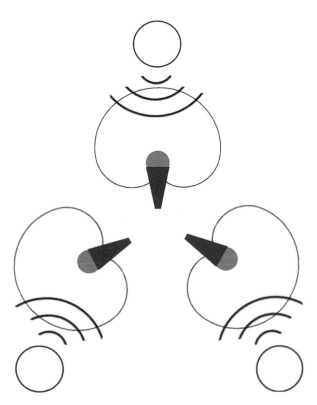

Figure 3.4 Three-mic setup.

unwanted source, then it should be something you can remedy or at least minimise when you are mixing the show later.

You can reduce bleed further by keeping your voices and microphones as far apart as is practical in the recording space. Obviously if you are in a large space, don't put them so far apart they have to shout to hear each other; but the further apart they are, then the lower the bleed.

Always use a pop shield on speech

First rule. Never forget your wind shield. It is possible to get a good recording without one but the speaker has to think pretty hard about their positioning. They're also a useful way to keep speakers from getting too close to the microphone if you use the kind of pop shield that is positioned between the mic and the speaker attached to the stand.

If you do forget a pop shield, avoid speaking directly into the microphone. Position it pointing slightly off-axis from the mouth to avoid the plosive blasts of air.

The six-inch rule

This will save you so much time and coaching. The six-inch rule is a really simple way to remember how to position yourself in front of a microphone. All you need to do is the "hang-ten" hand gesture and put the microphone at the end of your little finger with your thumb where your mouth should be (Figure 3.5).

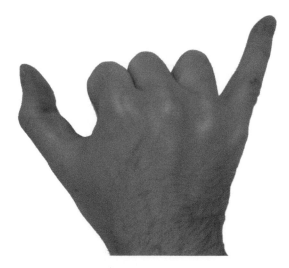

Figure 3.5 "Hang Ten" – a useful way to set the correct distance from a mic.

It's so easy to show this to guests as part of your pre-show chat and they will usually understand it easily and remember for the duration of their interview.

This also isn't a hard and fast rule. Your speakers don't need to hover exactly six inches from the mic, it is just something to tell them about and to keep in mind while recording.

Line of sight

This is only partly about audio quality, and mainly about the quality of your interview content. People like to be able to see each other properly when they are talking, and if your microphone is in the way, then the natural reaction is to lean around the microphone.

Having uncomfortable guests and show hosts probably isn't going to lead to a great interview. More importantly, if they are leaning around the microphone to see each other, then they aren't talking into that microphone. The mic is no longer pointing at where the sound comes from!

One workaround is to take advantage of the 3D nature of sound to place your microphones below your contributors' eyeline and have the point upwards, or you can have the mics off to one side. This might lead to you compromising your initial audio quality slightly by introducing a little more bleed; however, it won't be as bad as if your contributors feel the need to lean around the mics.

Proximity effect

The proximity effect is an increase in the bass when a voice gets really close to a directional microphone. The closer a voice gets to a microphone, the more pronounced the weight low end becomes. Lots of producers and engineers will consider this unintentional or degraded sound quality. However, some voice-over artists and hosts will actually lean into the mic to get a more bassy sound, creating a richer tone in their voice. It can be quite a nice effect, depending on the voice of the speaker.

The proximity effect can also drown out some of the crisp low ends though, muddying the sound and removing some vocal definition. It's not something that usually ruins audio, just a good thing to be aware of when you are recording.

Roll off

Some microphones have the option to take out frequencies below a certain level. There will usually be a small switch on the mic that looks a little like this (Figure 3.6):

Figure 3.6 High pass filter on a mic.

This is a roll off or high pass filter. It is used to remove the very low rumble end of the frequencies. This can take out ground noise from, for example, chairs rolling around or passing cars, all of which will drive your overall recording level up with noise you don't want.

Essentially, this means that in a space with lots of unwanted low end, you would have to set your overall recording level lower, so you can take out some low end in order to get a slightly higher overall sound.

It also means you have eliminated those frequencies from your recording permanently. You can't put frequencies back in once they are taken out, so you need to be sure you don't want the bass frequencies you are removing.

The roll off can also be used to counteract the proximity effect.

Multiple microphones

When recording multiple microphones, you should aim to have them as far apart from each other as is feasible within the space and comfortable for your speakers, and pointing in different directions. This will minimise the amount of bleed you get.

What is bleed?

Bleed is when your microphone records something other than the source it is intended to record. It is inevitable when you have multiple sound sources/speakers being recorded in the same room. It's something that is dealt with in editing, but you want to minimise it so that it isn't a problem when, for example, two speakers talk over each other.

Handheld microphones

If you are recording out of the studio, then at some point you will likely have to make do without a mic stand. Either your host and guest will be holding the mics or you will be doing some of the holding.

The six-inch rule still applies here, but you can be a little looser. The further from the speaker you are, the more background noise you will get. This might be desirable, if you want to capture the ambiance of an area. Alternately, you could use two microphones with one held nice and close to the speaker and another being used to capture atmosphere.

The key is consistency. Try and keep the microphone the same relative position to the speaker to avoid noticeable changes in a voice's volume, relative to background noise.

Make sure the microphone isn't held with the hand covering the grill. Some people do this because they've seen it in music videos and maybe it looks kind of cool, but you'll get muffled sound.

Don't point the microphone directly at the speaker's mouth and you'll avoid popping. It's totally fine to hold the mic below and slightly in front of your head, pointing upwards (Figure 3.7).

Figure 3.7 Handheld mic technique.

Hit record

You've pointed your microphones in the right direction and plugged everything into the right sockets. There is just a little bit more to go before you're ready to press record.

Before we get there, you have to make sure you are recording at the right level.

Too loud and you will get distorted audio, known as clipping. Clipping is when the signal amplitude is too high so it gets "clipped" off, creating a flat topped waveform, and it sounds awful when you play it back.

Too quiet, and you will have too much noise on the recording compared to the desired audio. This is referred to as a poor "signal to noise ratio" (SNR).

Gain staging

Set your gains correctly on any preamps and audio interfaces. You want the signal to be at a high enough level at every stage that any noise introduced is not noticeable compared to the audio, but not so high it distorts or clips. On most equipment with a gain control, there will be a meter that goes from green, to yellow, to red. Aim to be in the yellow, but leave enough room that it won't go into the red when someone laughs or raises their voice.

To set your gain:

9   Turn your gain control right down, then get your speaker to talk into the microphone and gradually turn it up until you get a good signal level without going over and clipping.
10   Make sure you listen to the signal to pick up on any audible clipping or other problems.

If you are the producer and not the host, then I find it easiest to get the host and guest to just sit and chat to warm up before the actual interview, and I set gains during this. That way, you get the natural conversation volume. Lots of people go artificially loud or quiet when they are consciously saying "test test".

It is better to be a little too quiet than a little too loud. It's much easier to raise level later than it is to remove a lot of clipping.

In your DAW software

If you don't have them already create a channel for each microphone. These should be mono channels – one microphone provides one audio signal. Make sure the inputs are correct.

In Adobe Audition you can find the input setting on the multitrack mixer at the top of each channel (Figure 3.8).

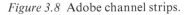

Figure 3.8 Adobe channel strips.

You will also have to check that your recording levels are fine in your software – take a look at the metres on your recording channel while your speakers are chatting before the interview and make sure it isn't clipping. If it is hitting the red, then check for anywhere that additional gain could be applied, such as the output of the preamp, and bring it down a little until the metres aren't in the red. The better you know your equipment, the easier you will find this.

If you're recording to a portable recorder

Some recorders have an auto gain setting. These are super useful if you just need to get going quickly, and in my experience have been pretty good at avoiding any clipping.

If you don't have an auto setting, then, as above, make sure your gain is set to an appropriate level. This might be called "Rec Level" in the recorder's menu.

OK, now you can hit record!

Pro tip: get to this point well before your speakers are actually ready to go and start recording before the "official" start of the interview. You never know what you might want to keep and use later!

Field recordings

Recording outside of a controlled environment like a studio or your own living space is definitely more challenging. It's also much more varied and fun. Importantly, this is where you will get texture-rich recordings to really liven up a podcast. This section is especially important if you are going to make documentaries.

Working with background noise

When you are recording outside or in busier environments, there is going to be background noise. That's OK! Don't try and get rid of it. It brings a listener into the space with you. It can really create a sense of place. If you are producing documentary-style podcasts, especially background noise can be used to indicate movement and transport the listener to the different places you have visited.

You do have to know how to work with it though. Make sure your speakers are close enough to the microphones that they are significantly louder and more present than the background noise.

Record some **Wildtrack**. You might also hear this referred to as **Room Tone**, especially if you are in the USA. Take a minute or so just to record the background noise of the space you are in with nobody speaking. You can use this to cover edits later on, or even to run under some voice-over when you want to give the impression of a location. This is important to gather even in spaces that seem quiet, because even the quietest space has its own ambient sounds. If you want your speech to be completely devoid of background noise, then it is still necessary to gather wildtrack. Most noise reduction software either requires or operates better if you have gathered wildtrack to feed its algorithm.

Pay attention to the characteristic sounds of the space. In a train station, this might be announcements or a passing train. In summer in North America, you might hear cicadas buzzing away, fading in and out. Take some time to just listen and record things that you want to work with. The more you practice this, the quicker you will be able to pinpoint sounds and figure out what wildtrack you need for your edit.

Your wildtrack shouldn't have any particularly distinct sounds, such as intelligible conversation or one lonely car horn. If you're using it in your edit later, you don't want it to distract from the interview or voice-over.

You can also use an additional microphone just to record the background noise, especially if you have a super close range directional microphone for the speakers. This is a little trickier at the recording stage, but allows you to set the balance a little better in the mixing stage.

And as always, don't forget the wind shield on every microphone!

Listen

It's always important to monitor your recording as it is happening, but in an unpredictable environment it is especially important to keep your ears on your audio. Pay close attention to background noise and whether your speakers are sitting clearly above it.

Don't forget

Batteries. Bring twice as many as you need, you really don't want to run out.

Cables. Always bring spares. Cables break easily.

Storage. Make sure you have some extra SD cards in case you need to record more than planned or the one you planned on using corrupts.

Backups

Equipment fails. No matter how expensive it is or how well you take care of it, sometimes things go wrong.

So, you should have a backup. Depending on how kitted out you are, this can look like a lot of different things. The full belt and braces approach would be to run two recorders with two sets of microphones recording the same thing... but for most people this is overkill. A good alternative is to have a second portable recorder roughly in between the guests recording the interview just using the built-in microphones. The quality obviously won't be as good as your main recording, but if something dies you still have the interview.

If you don't have access to two recorders but you do have a smartphone just set that down on the table and start the recorder app going. On iPhones, this is called Voice Memo and on Android it is called Recorder.

Equipment

There is a whole section on microphone choice earlier in this book, but choosing the right gear is even more important when you're working outside the studio. For recording in the field, you probably want microphones that are a little more durable and resistant to handling noise and for recording interviews on location, a couple of directional microphones. Try a cardioid polar pattern at first, and if you find there is too much background noise, move the microphones a little closer or try a tighter polar pattern such as super cardioid. Don't forget that if you're using condensers, you need phantom power from your recorder.

A good bag of kit for recording a variety of audio in the field will include the following at a minimum:

- A portable recorder with at least two XLR inputs and one headphone output
- Two cardioid microphones
- Two XLR cables (preferably more for redundancy)
- Wind shields for each microphone
- A pair of headphones
- Batteries
- SD Cards

The rugged Shure SM58 is a good choice if you're on a limited budget and want a durable microphone that can be used for a bunch of different types of recording in the field.

A more complete set could also have the following:

- A shotgun mic for recording a speaker in a noisy environment.
- One or two omnidirectional mics for gathering ambient noise.
- Portable microphone stands. Small stands that can be set up on a table are very useful for avoiding handling noise and are more comfortable for long interviews.
- Two or even three pairs of headphones for a producer, host and guest.
- A headphone chord splitter, if your recorder doesn't have a second headphone output.
- A second portable recorder to run as a backup.
- Waterproof case for recording in the rain (or in my case here in Canada... snow).

You probably don't want to be setting up laptops and audio interfaces outside, so a portable recorder really is essential for location recordings. Zoom makes a recorder that will record up to 8 tracks at once for under $400, in case you feel like doing anything a little more complex.

Weather

Rain is an obvious problem. You don't need a book to tell you to cover your electrical equipment when water is falling from the sky. The climate can affect your recording in other perhaps unexpected ways though.

The temperature will change how your batteries work. In sub-zero temperatures, the chemical reaction inside a battery can slow down so much that it doesn't emit enough charge to keep a device working, so wrap your equipment up and don't keep it out in the cold too long. Don't attempt to charge any rechargeable batteries in this situation – despite the reading on your equipment, they are probably still full of charge, the batteries just aren't able to emit that charge.

Heat will have the opposite effect on the battery and speed up the chemical reaction. The end result is the same for you though – a dead battery. So if you're working in temperatures over 30°C, keep your gear in the shade and carry spare batteries. In any weather don't put your equipment close to heat sources.

And while we are on weather... I've said it before, I'll say it again. Don't forget your wind shields. Wind can ruin a recording so easily. You really don't want to have to do your recording sheltering behind a car and hoping a big gust doesn't wreck your interview.

Studio etiquette: how not to break your stuff or your staff

Let's try not to break anything or anyone while we are making podcasts. Really, stick with me through this bit. You'll regret it if you don't and have to buy a whole new set of equipment (or a new assistant producer) because you broke them.

Noise levels

You really do not want tinnitus or hearing loss when you work in audio, so watch how loud your speakers and headphones are set.

I mean every single pair of headphones and speakers.

To avoid blowing anyone's ears out, make turning the volume on everything down to zero part of your routine when you are first using a studio. Then, slowly raise them up while some audio is playing out until you get them to a comfortable level. You might be working with these levels for hours, so keep it reasonable. If you have to raise your voice to talk over it, then it is too loud.

Every pair of headphones should be turned right down until some-one puts them on, then gradually raise them up while asking that person to signal when they want you to stop. This isn't just a safety thing – headphones that are turned on without being pressed to someone's head could be picked up on a microphone causing feedback or unwanted noise on the recording.

If you do turn the speakers up to check how something sounds loud, keep it short.

Trip hazards

With cables running everywhere, it is easy to create trip hazards. You want to do everything you can to minimise this risk.

Use longer cables than necessary and loop the extra length at the base of the microphone stand. This way, there is some slack should some-body's foot get caught:

• Run cables around the edge of rooms or equipment where possible.
• Avoid running cables in places where people are most likely to walk.
• Try to keep multiple cables bunched together to create one obvious point to step over.
• If you have some, tape cables to the floor or place mats over cable runs.
• Use brightly coloured cables. As a bonus, this makes it easier to remember which is which if you have multiple colours!

Cable coiling

If you want instant respect from a sound engineer, all you have to do is pick up a cable and coil it properly. Follow this guide on tidying away cables and you'll swiftly be invited into the black t-shirt club.

Cables might appear thick and sturdy thanks to the chunky rubber casing, but they are still just thin bits of copper inside their thick skin. That copper can fray and break pretty easily, and the rubber of the casing remembers how it has been twisted so easily develops kinks and knots.

To counter this, we use a technique called the over/under technique.

I'm going to use "primary" and "secondary" here when talking about which hand to use. If you are right-handed, then your right is your pri-mary hand and your left is your secondary hand.

Before you coil a cable, run it through your hands once to make sure there are no knots or kinks (Figure 3.9).

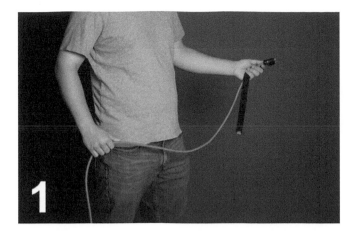

Figure 3.9 Coiling a cable step 1.

1   Take the connector and point it away from yourself with your secondary thumb resting along the cable, pointing towards the connector (Figure 3.10).

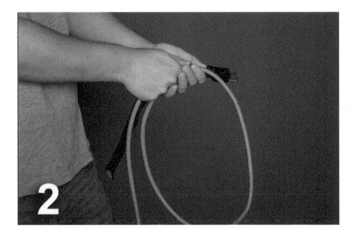

Figure 3.10 Coiling a cable step 2.

2   Take the loose part of the cable in your primary hand and point that thumb in the same direction (Figure 3.11).

Figure 3.11 Coiling a cable step 3.

3   Pull your primary hand back along the cable, giving it a slight twist inwards to loop it back into a circle. This is the "over" part of the over/under.

4   Now, for the second loop do the same, except twisting in the opposite direction. To make this feel more natural, point your primary thumb downwards before doing the coil. This is the "under" loop (Figure 3.12).

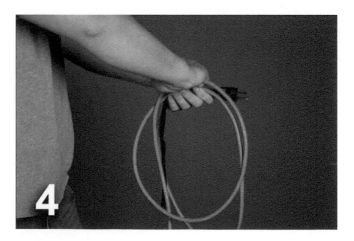

Figure 3.12 Coiling a cable step 4.

Do that until you have a coiled cable, and then use a cable tidy to secure it.

This probably seems like a lot to learn just to put cables away, but it will save you a lot of time with your cables in the long run. Turning up for a recording and spending 15 minutes untangling a knot of cables only to find out that one of them isn't working doesn't make you look particularly professional, not to mention how annoying and cost-inefficient it is.

Don't tie your cables in knots to finish off the loop. You will break them, if not on the first knot, then somewhere down the line.

Drinks

Drink some water, you dehydrated podcast noodle.

… but you are surrounded by expensive microphones and electronic equipment that, when mixed with liquids, could lead to a *shockingly* bad recording; so don't do anything silly like putting your glass down on top of a preamp or keeping your coffee next to a power outlet. You could get electrocuted, start a fire or just break some expensive gear.

Mic stands and heavy equipment

Just be careful not to hit anyone with that long metal pole you are swinging around. Some stands are heavy as well, so lift with your knees not your back.

Move, noodle

When you're deep in an edit, it is really easy to lose track of time. Suddenly you have been hunched in the same chair for six hours, your neck hurts, your back is crooked and your mouse finger is cramped.

Just make sure you get up and wiggle around once an hour or so. Taking a break from listening helps reset your ears as well. You'll probably notice ear fatigue if you've been working for a long time.

Oh yeah, ear fatigue

Like any part of your body, your ears get tired when you use them for a long time. This is especially noticeable when you're mixing – you will start to question whether the equaliser (EQ) or compression you're applying is actually making your audio sound better or not. You sort of lose your baseline for audio quality. Take a break, don't listen to anything in particular for a while. Get out the studio and walk around to reset.

When you get back from your break, listen to something else for a bit to re-establish a baseline for what produced audio should sound like.

Remote recording and double-enders

What if I told you that most interviews aren't recorded face to face? That was true before the coronavirus came around and changed the way we produce, and it is even more true now.

Knowing how to get a good quality recording from your interviewee when they don't have any recording equipment or a great space for recording in is an important skill. It requires a degree of coaching your interviewee and the ability to take educated guesses when troubleshooting.

Don't get me wrong, a face-to-face interview in a good studio will still get you the best interview. The sound quality of a professional space and the intimacy of in-person conversation can't be beat, but let's be real here and accept that you are going to need to interview people for whom it is unrealistic to be physically in the same place.

One method for doing this is called a tape sync, and we'll cover that in more detail in a series of exercises throughout this book. That's where you hire a producer who is near to your guest to go and record them for you while you interview them over the phone or on a video call. That's what the bigger organisations tend to do when they want to ensure quality audio; however, you need to pay a producer for this and it's not always possible to get someone at short notice.

So we need to know how to coach a guest to get a good recording themselves. This is a double-ender.

What we are doing with both a tape sync and a double-ender is making two totally separate recordings, each made locally to one of the people speaking. We'll sync the two bits of audio up later in the edit.

There needs to be a way for the interviewer and interviewee to hear each other as well, which is going to be totally unrelated to the recordings. This can be something like Zoom or Skype, or even just a phone call.

Recording the guest with a phone

Most people have a smartphone, and most smartphones already have a recording app built in. The microphone in an iPhone is actually really good.

This phone is not for making a call from. It should be in airplane mode. You are just using it as a convenient replacement for a portable recorder, as most people don't have one of those lying around.

As tempting as it is to just record your guest's video chat at the host end, you'll be glad you did it this way when it gets to editing. A local recording avoids any glitches and dropouts caused by internet connection and will be better quality audio than the compressed, thin sound of most video chat software.

In Android the recording app is called "Recorder". In iPhones it is called "Voice Memo". Both have a similar method of operating – you open up the app, hit record. When you're done, hit stop and give it a name. Then you tap and hold on the recording and hit share to send it. It's pretty self-explanatory. You can share the file however you like – Dropbox, Google Drive, whatever your guest is comfortable with. These might be long files though, so straight up email probably isn't an option.

Play around with both the Android Recorder and iPhone Voice Memo until you are comfortable with both, so that if your guest has any issues you are able to help them out. I often get the guest to switch to WAV format in the apps settings (the little cog logo) in order to get the best quality possible.

So that is how you get a recording. Now let's look at how you get a **good** recording.

Do:

11 Hold the phone like a phone (Figure 3.13).

Figure 3.13 Phone to head.

Phone microphones are designed to be used with the phone held stuck to your ear, so that is where they get the best quality. It is really tempting to place it in front of your mouth, but that will give you a lot of plosive noises and probably some clipping too:

- Put the phone into airplane mode. Calls will interrupt the recording, and you don't want noises from text messages or other alerts on there either.
- Make sure the phone is adequately charged – generally at least 50% for an hour-long recording.
- Close windows, draw curtains and choose a quiet room... if you've read the chapter "turn any space into a studio", you can pass on lot of the tips in that chapter to your guests.
- Turn off appliances, especially air conditioning.
- Hold the phone as still as possible.
- Pause for interruptions, so that they can be edited out easily.

Don't:

- Use airpods or other bluetooth headsets; the audio quality from these is often terrible.
- Put the phone on speakerphone. The recording will have the host's low quality call back down the line.
- Treat the phone like a regular microphone (Figure 3.14).

Holding the phone this way will introduce plosives and distortion to the final recording.

- Change the position of the phone during the interview.

If you have multiple guests, even if they're in the same room get them to record themselves separately into separate phones. Two people attempting to talk into the same microphone is going to sound messy, and to get a good quality recording they would have to be... uncomfortably close. To make life easier in editing, get someone to clap once the recordings have started, giving you a sharp transient to use as a sync point later, just like using a clapper board in film.

If your guest wants to use their *wired* headset to record with (not wireless! Avoid wireless!), then they may be able to, and it will help them avoid a tired arm for the duration of the interview. However, make sure they do an audio test with you beforehand and remove any clothing or jewellery that could catch on the cable. The guest fatigue here could come from the need to sit pretty still to avoid rustling noises on the headset – they're pretty prone to that, and you don't notice it so much when you are just

Figure 3.14 Bad phone technique.

on a call with someone, but in a podcast, where you aren't talking back and are actively listening, the handling noise can get quite distracting if too present.

Much like the iPhone, Apple's headset has a decent quality micro-phone in it…. And much like the iPhone, you shouldn't try and get clever with positioning it. Have them put one earbud in and let it dangle, as they would when using the headset for hands-free calls.

They only put one earbud in because, as this phone isn't being used for the call, they won't hear anything from it and need to keep another ear free for the call. Make sure they don't knock, fiddle with or touch the cable while recording, as it is sensitive to handling noise.

Do a test before the interview

Before it comes to the actual recording send your guest all the infor-mation they need on how to get a good recording. They will inevitably ignore most of what you've told them, so get them to do a test recording using the same equipment and space that they'll do the interview in.

Here are a few common issues that you might hear in the audio and solutions you can try out:

- Sounds like a telephone line – they are probably using a bluetooth headset such as airpods. Get them to switch these off and just speak into the phone.
- Low fidelity audio, especially if the audio received is *.AMR or *.OGG format – get them to go into the settings in their recorder app and switch to WAV or at least MP3 if it is available.
- Plosives – distortion on "p", "t", "d" and "b" sounds. They are likely holding the phone wrong, directly in front of their mouth. Switch to holding the phone to their ear, as in the diagram above.
- Humming sounds in the background – they may be sitting near an air conditioning unit or other appliances. Have them turn these off or change location.
- Tapping sounds – they may be handling the headset cable.
- Muffled audio, especially lacking low end – their hand or a phone case may be covering the microphone.
- Excessively reverberant (or echoey) audio – they may be holding the phone too far away from their mouth. If that's not the case, they should try closing curtains or changing the room they are in.

Record yourself

Set up your microphone as you would for any other recording and record yourself locally and entirely separately from the call. You should have a clean recording with just your own microphone on it.

You could also use your portable recorder entirely separate to the computer. If you do this, make sure you do a separate soundcheck and monitor the audio quality.

Connect

Of course, you and your guest need to be able to hear each other. Being able to see your interviewee can help too, so most people connect with a video call using something like Zoom, Skype or Google Hangouts.

This is separate to your recording and is just there as a communication tool; however, you should definitely also record the video chat audio as a backup. There are plenty of apps that will record this, such as Total Recorder in Windows or Audio Hijack in Apple OS. Zoom also allows you to record the audio right in the app.

If your guest doesn't have a good internet connection, then a phone line will work just fine. Tip: you can use Skype to call phones internationally with a subscription that is about $5 a month, and this lets you record the phone line as a backup easily within your computer the same as you would record any video chat.

Ideally, your guest should use headphones for the video call, so that your own voice doesn't appear on their recording. If they're using a headset to record into the phone, they might find it uncomfortable to wear two separate earbuds though and you'll just have to sort that out in the edit, and hopefully both speakers avoid talking over each other.

Being able to see your guest really does help you coach them through their technique with the phone though, so I would recommend a video call where possible.

Before you get started, make sure you remind them to hit record.

Send the audio

Once you're done, get them to hit stop and then share and they can use their preferred method to send you the audio. If they aren't used to sharing large files, you might have to talk them through using something like Dropbox, Google Drive or WeTransfer to send it to you.

Syncing it up for the edit

Once you have both parts of the interview, drop them into your Digital Audio Workstation (DAW) on individual mono tracks (if they are in stereo, split them down to mono – it will save you some processor power). You and your guest will have started recording at different times, so you need to line them up. This should be pretty easy – there will be gaps in guest's track where your host asks the questions and vice versa.

If there is audio bleed, for example, if your guest has had the host coming out of the laptop speakers, you can actually use this to line up your tracks much more precisely. Zoom right in and match up some peaks on each line (Figure 3.15).

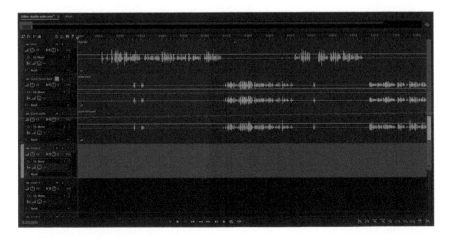

Figure 3.15 Adobe sync.

In more conversational interviews where the two participants might speak over each other, you really want the audio to match up exactly, so take some time to listen to particular exchanges and make sure it sounds right.

High-quality audio connections

If your guest has a good microphone and you trust both your internet connections, you can also record using one of the specialist VOIP software that are designed especially for recording podcasts. They need a little more expertise from the producer and are less forgiving of the equipment.

Skype, Zoom and Google Hangouts all have heavy audio compression and ducking algorithms built into them that kind of ruins the sound quality but does help the connection stay stable and avoids feedback. They're designed to be idiot proof. Luckily, we know a bit more than most about audio by now, so we can switch to something more sophisticated.

These apps replace your regular video chat software, so don't allow video to save bandwidth and attempt to provide audio at much higher quality. For this to work well, you need to make sure everyone is using headphones, avoiding feedback. You should also have good internet connections and a good microphone too.

Some examples of these types of app are:

- IPDTL
- Clearcast
- Zencastr
- Squadcast

If you can't be sure everyone speaking has a good microphone, headphones and solid internet connection, then you should stick with self-recording on a smartphone, or try both with the phone as a backup.

This type of recording is ideal when you have two hosts that need to record some chit-chat together and can invest in a good setup at each end.

You will use this chapter more than you think in your podcast production. It is rare for a producer to have the budget to travel to faraway places just to grab a half hour of audio, so whether it is just grabbing short clips for documentaries or for lengthy feature interviews, it pays to know how to get good audio whether you can be there in person or not.

Exercise: remote recording, part 1

Most interviews are not recorded face to face, and remote recording became even more normalised during the COVID-19 pandemic. We covered how to make do with limited resources in the last chapter, but some of the bigger and more professional production operations will want to ensure they get good audio quality. To make absolutely sure of that you can't leave it up to your guest to get a quality recording, you need to send a professional.

If you're looking to get your foot in the door and get paid for some relatively simple podcast work, then you want to be that professional that they send. It's a good way to show you know your basics and that you're trustworthy.

This is an especially useful skill if you live somewhere that isn't one of the major media hub cities of London, New York, LA and Toronto. If you're somewhere that still has people to be interviewed but isn't full of production companies, then that's your first selling point as a tape sync.

This is the quality version of a double-ender, and it is usually referred to as a **Tape Sync**.

So let's learn how to be a trustworthy tape syncer, so that when those opportunities come up you're ready to grab your gear and earn your first buck in the world of professional audio production. Throughout this book are exercises that will help you prepare for a tape sync and execute it flawlessly when you get there.

A tape sync follows the same principle as the double-ender described in the previous chapter. Two separate recordings are made, one at each location. The interviewer and interviewee communicate over the phone or video chat, which is separate to the recordings made.

When a producer hires someone to do a tape sync, they are hiring them to go to the location of their interviewee and record that interviewee's end of the conversation. The interviewer, whether that is a producer or host, is recording their own end, probably in a studio (and if they're being cautious, they record the Skype/phone as a backup.)

You'll use your own equipment, and a lot of the techniques covered already in this book.

It's up to you how you do the recording, but most people will bring the following as a minimum:

Gear

12 Portable recorder
13 One dynamic microphone, cardioid polar pattern
14 One condenser microphone, cardioid polar pattern

• If you have microphone stands, bring them. Your arm might get tired holding a microphone in place for a long time

15 Cables and batteries

If you have a good way of making a backup recording such as a second recorder, bring that too and put it to use. You're being paid for this after all and don't want to let your employers down.

Arriving

Turn up with enough time before the recording starts to scope out the venue and pick the best place to get set up. You are looking for somewhere with low reverb and not much ambient noise. Make sure you aren't going to be interrupted and turn off appliances like air conditioners.

Remember, this is likely the guest's home or office, so don't get too pushy with moving things around for the recording. Firm, polite competence is the key here.

You are a producer here, whether you intend to or not. You are probably the first person associated with the podcast that the guest has met in person, so it's up to you to be personable and put them in a good mindset for being interviewed.

Preparing

Test your equipment before you even set off for the tape sync. There's nothing worse than arriving to find your recorder has died.

Have the guest sit down and make sure they are comfortable – that way they won't be shifting all over the place during the interview itself. Set up the microphones and start recording as soon as the interviewer is connected – that way you definitely won't miss the start.

Tell anyone else in the house that you will be recording so that they can avoid interrupting you.

Walk around with your headphones plugged into the recorder so you can get a feel for where sounds best through the microphone. If you have the option of a couple of different microphones, try them out and see what works best in the room you are in.

Record some ambient room noise with nobody talking. Your producer might be able to use this for noise cancellation or edits when they are cutting the interview.

Once you are settled on a place, get your equipment set up and test it all out to make sure it's still working fine. Cables can easily get damaged in transit.

During the recording

Start your recorder as soon as the interviewer is connected to the interviewee. Sometimes producers like to use that early chit-chat as clips to set the scene, and you never know what you might get. It's also pretty common to not have a defined start to the interview and just slip seamlessly from conversation to interview. It helps keep the interview sounding conversational, so you don't want to wait for an "official start" to hit record.

Listen to the recording on your headphones so you can hear what is actually being recorded and identify any issues. Keep one eye on your recorder in case your batteries run low or storage space is running out.

In general, don't interrupt the recording, especially during particularly interesting parts; however, there are judgement calls to be made here.

Firmly, politely, interrupt the recording if there are any audible interruptions that have jeopardized the audio, but don't overdo it – sometimes it can take the interviewer a long time to get the interviewee into the right head space to get the answers that they want. This is why picking a quiet area and preparing properly to minimise interruptions is important.

Bear in mind the interviewer may be on a low-quality connection so might not hear things that your mic can pick up. Part of the art here is knowing when to interrupt and get the guest to restart what they were saying.

Hold the mic steady. Don't get right up in your guest's face – you'll both feel uncomfortable with that – but don't let them get too far away from the mic either. Be careful of handling noise.

Remember, this isn't your interview. You're acting as a location engineer, not a producer or interviewer here.

After the recording

Remember to hit stop, double check the audio is saved by playing it back before leaving.

It might be tempting to edit out any mistakes you made – cutting plosives, for example; however, this will cause small differences in the duration of the two recordings and make the producer's edit harder. You should instead make note of any problems with the recording, including time codes if it's practical, and send those to the producer with the recording you made.

Make sure to send them the recordings as soon as possible and keep a backup of the file too.

Tape sync exercise 1

For this exercise let's do a mock tape sync recording, so you can confidently turn up for your first paid gig and know what you're doing.

Pick a friend or family member to record. Don't tell them in advance what you need from them or what kind of space you want to record in – you might not get the chance to do so in a real tape sync situation, depending on the producer!

The point of this exercise is to get a feel for scoping out the venue and get the best quality recording possible with what's available. You should be able to use what you learned in the chapter "turn any space into a studio" to good effect here.

Get a friend to call your "guest" to conduct an "interview" so that you know what it is like to be the third person in a two-person interview.

Have them record themselves at the other end too – you'll need this for exercise 3.

First, do a recording without taking any of the preparation steps above. You only really need to record a minute or so of audio here, there's no need to sit down for a full half hour interview.

Second, go through all the steps and use all the knowledge you've gained in this book so far to get the best possible audio with what is available and do another recording.

Now, compare the two and listen to the difference!

We'll pick up with some more exercises later in the book, so you can see what it's like to be on the other end of a tape sync as well.

Quick start guide

You are jumping into the studio and you don't have time to read that whole chapter? OK, no worries. I've got you covered, and here are the basics.

1 Point the microphone where the sound comes from

16 Get your microphones set up six inches or a hand's length away from your speakers' mouths.
17 Have your speakers as far apart as possible, but facing each other.
18 Make sure they are the right way round: the manufacturer's logo is usually the front of the microphone. Point this at the mouth.
19 Make sure you have pop shields on the mics.
20 Set the polar pattern to cardioid.
21 Plug them into your recording gear with XLR cables.

2 Set your gain

• Have your speakers talk into their mics.
• Adjust the gain controls on your equipment until the level meters are mostly in the yellow, but never hitting red. In deciBels Full Scale (dBfs) this is probably around the –15 to –5 range. Too high and you will get clipping distortion, too low and the signal to noise ratio will be poor.
• Listen and make sure it sounds good – you are checking for distortion, popping, echo and background hums and noise:

3 Troubleshoot

What's wrong? Nothing? Are you sure? Listen really carefully. If everything sounds fine, skip this and go to number 4.

• Distorted, fuzzy audio, especially when voices are raised: your gain is too high. Turn it down until the distortion doesn't happen.

- Low pitched hum: swap out your cables; if that doesn't work, swap out your microphone. Keep equipment away from mains power sources.
- Feedback:

  A loud howling/ringing sound: is anything feeding the audio from the microphones back into the microphones, such as monitors or loose headphones? Perhaps your guests' headphones are too loud.

  Low-level noise from the headphones, such as producer talkback: turn the headphones down.
- Too much echo: check your mic positioning. Reposition them and your speakers so that they aren't pointed at any flat surfaces such as glass. Draw any curtains. Make sure the mics are six inches from the speakers.
- There is a "popping" blast of distortion on plosive sounds like "p", "d" and "b": make sure your pop shields are fitted to the microphones. Adjust the microphone positioning so that it isn't directly in front of the speakers' mouths, for example, just off to the side but still pointing at the mic.
- Voice is too bass heavy: this could be the proximity effect, have your speaker move *away* from the mic slightly.
- Too much room sound: move the microphones *closer* to the speakers.
- Rumbling sounds in the lower end: could be from cars driving past outside or people walking around causing the stand to shake a little. If your microphone has a rolloff setting, switch it on, otherwise this can be removed later.
- You're getting too much "bleed", unwanted noise from the other sound sources in the studio: try moving the microphones further apart. However, with multiple sound sources in the same space, you will always have some bleed that has to be edited out in post-production. Just make sure that a microphone gets much more of its intended sound source than anything else through effective positioning.

4 Press record

- Your job isn't done though! Keep monitoring the recording. Make sure it doesn't stop unexpectedly (computers are awkward aren't they?). All of the issues covered in the troubleshooting section can occur during the recording too.
- **Listen, actively**. Not only will you notice any technical issues but you'll find your edit easier later because you'll already know what was interesting and what wasn't.

5 Stop. Save. Save a backup

Congratulations, you've recorded something! I bet it's great. Let's listen to it and figure out how we edit it to make it even better shall we?

4   Editing

Introduction to editing

Editing is one of the things that separate a recording technician from a producer. It's the difference between a meandering conversation with awkward pauses and a slick podcast interview.

Listeners will tell you that they want authenticity and unedited conversations. That's because they usually don't get to hear how tedious and long-winded unedited conversations can be. This chapter is going to show you how to cut out the boring parts.

It's not just large chunks you'll want to remove. Listeners also don't get to hear just how, frankly, disgusting an intimate recording of a human mouth is and just how much "umming" and "aahhing" people tend to do when they speak. We're going to remove all of that filler as well.

Editing is an art form, both on an editorial level and a technical level. You never finish learning how to edit. That might sound daunting but the best time to start learning is now, and the basics are really easy to pick up.

On a technical level, there are two types of editing we are going to talk about in this chapter: destructive and non-destructive.

Destructive editing is editing the actual audio file itself. Any edits made are final as soon as you hit save. This is how most single waveform editors work. You should always keep a backup when working this way.

Non-destructive editing doesn't alter the audio file. Most multitrack editors work this way, with "clips" acting as editable windows into the audio they are looking at.

You'll use both as you put a podcast together, but non-destructive will definitely make up the lion's share of the work.

On a non-technical level, there are a few kinds of editing as well, although the lines are a little more blurry:

- **Top and tail**: cutting down the pre-interview and post-interview off. The most basic edit, leaving everything internal intact.
- **Content editing**: selecting the parts you want to stay in based on their editorial merit and your own time goals.
- **Clean-up:** removing unnecessary pauses and gross mouth noises.

DOI: 10.4324/9781003046578-4

Where to start

You've gathered your interviews and field recordings. You've recorded your voice-over. You've picked out some music. Now you have to actually put it all together.

That's a lot of raw audio… where do we begin?

Interviews are the core of most podcasts, so let's start with how to edit an interview.

Before we get started on the actual editing process, let's have a quick look at the tools you'll be using in most editors. I'll use Adobe Audition as an example, but all editors use some variation of these tools.

Clips

All multitrack editors make use of clips in some way or another. These are the representation of your audio files in the multitrack window. To understand what they are doing, I visualise each clip as a window through which you can "see" part of the audio. When you edit a clip in the multitrack, you aren't changing the audio underneath… you are changing the size and position of the window (Figure 4.1).

Tools

These replace your regular mouse cursor:

- Move tool: this is the "default" mouse cursor and works similarly to your regular computer mouse cursor. You pick up and drag clips around the multitrack view to arrange them. You can also shorten and lengthen clips.
- Razor: clicking creates a cut in the audio clip at the cursor position. You use this when working in the multitrack view to separate clips into two, allowing them to be moved and edited independently of one another.
- Time selection: clicking and dragging allows you to select all audio within an area. This is particularly useful in the waveform editor view in Adobe audition, allowing you to play specific sections before you make destructive cuts.

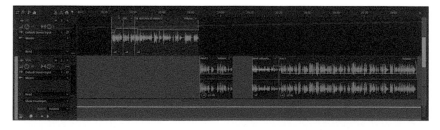

Figure 4.1 Adobe clips.

Other really useful functions

• Group: this isn't in your list of tools but is a really important function that you'll make a lot of use of. This lets you group clips together so that if you move one of them, you move all of them. The Razor will cut across all grouped clips that are vertically aligned Edits to the start, and the end of vertically aligned grouped clips will be synced up too.

Tip: set a key command for "select all clips to end of session" and "select all clips to start of session". This way, you can easily select and group all audio clips to the left or right of your cursor.

• Ripple Delete: this will delete your selection without leaving a gap in the multitrack. You can achieve the same thing by grouping everything to the right of your selection, deleting the selection and then moving it with the move tool, but this will just save you a few steps. In Pro-Tools, this is called "Slip Mode".

Those are the tools, here's how to use them.

First steps

Create a session

Open up your Digital Audio Workstation (DAW). Adobe Audition is an industry standard, so we are going to stick with that for this guide, but the steps will be the same in other apps too. The menus might look a little different, but the same procedures exist in Pro-Tools, Reaper and others.

In Adobe, click file > new > multitrack session. You'll be presented with a window like this (Figure 4.2):

You should know what to pick here if you've read the rest of this book, but a good standard is a sample rate of 48,000hz and a bit depth of 24. This is broadcast standard for radio, but you can work at 44,100Hz and 16-bit without a big loss in quality.

Get your formats right

Start by making sure your audio is in the right format. If you've been doing remote recordings, it's likely your interviewees may send you a stereo file in M4A or similar. It's good practice to always work in WAV where possible. You can't undo compression but you can prevent audio being re-compressed multiple times, degrading it further. You should also split any speech that is in stereo to a mono file. In Adobe Audition this is really

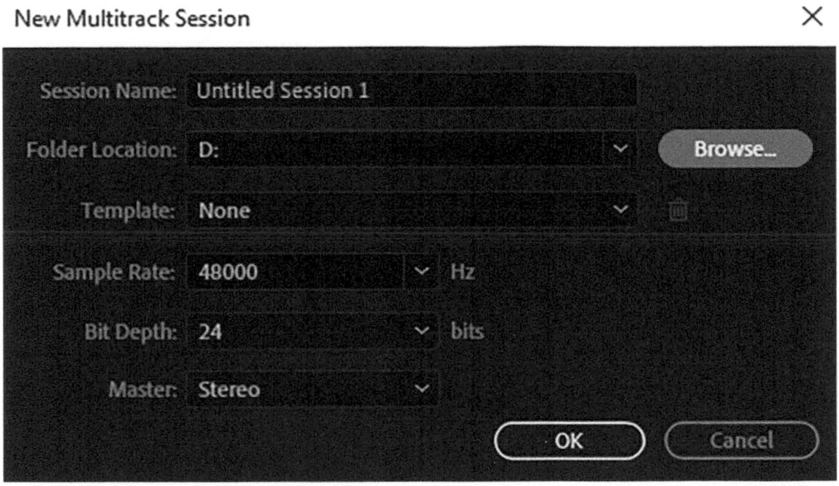

New Multitrack Session ✕

Session Name:	Untitled Session 1
Folder Location:	D:
Template:	None
Sample Rate:	48000 Hz
Bit Depth:	24 bits
Master:	Stereo

OK   Cancel

Figure 4.2 New multitrack session.

simple: right click on the file in the files pool to the left of the screen and select "extract channels to mono files".

Adobe will convert your files to the right format when you drag them into the session, so long as you make sure they are in mono you can let the software do the work here.

Sync them up

Line up each file from an interview on its own mono track in the multi-track editor. Zoom right in when you're doing this to get the files in sync down to the millisecond. At this point, you should export a "raw" edit of the interview that you can use for transcribing. It's also not a bad idea to keep this archived.

The stages of an edit

We'll cover the more technical aspects of editing a little later in the book. For now, these are the stages that your interview edit will likely take.

You will find your own preferred way of working, but it's common to have one master multitrack session per episode and then a separate mul-titrack session for each interview edit. This keeps things a little neater and stops you accidentally making edits in your master project when all you want to do is something small within an interview.

Your master session will contain your voice-over tracks, music and any extra audio but your interview edit should only have the host and guest(s).

The rough cut

Before you get into really fine editing, you should figure out what it is you want to do. As you have your audio synced up, you can listen to the interview in full and figure out what you are going to keep and what you are going to get rid of.

A lot of producers transcribe their audio to text at this point. There are a bunch of different browser-based transcription software like Otter. ai and Trint that will do this for you. The more old school radio producer way of editing would be to do what is called a "paper edit" at this point, and go over the transcript marking what you think should stay or go – preferably while listening to the original audio to check that it sounds good too. Generally these are broad-brush edits, for example, if this is for an interview-focused podcast, you would be selecting the most interesting parts of an interview to stay and cutting the less engaging sections or removing any lengthy repetition. If it's a documentary, you might be finding the killer clips for your host to track voice-over around.

Once you have done the paper edit, you jump back into your DAW and make those edits real. There is no need for making them perfect at this stage, you are just knocking the interview into the rough shape you want it to be.

Tip: work from the end backwards; that way, any time codes and edit markers you have placed in the session stay accurate until you don't need them anymore.

A great time saver at this point is a piece of software called Descript. Descript transcribes the audio for you and then lets you edit it in the same way you would edit text in Microsoft Word or Google Docs, so you can do both the paper edit and the rough cut at the same time. Descript even lets you export the edit to an Adobe session, which is good because the edits it makes are often imperfect. You can also use the automated "remove filler words" function to get rid of a lot of "ums".

Once you've done this, take another listen to make sure it sounds good. Are there any continuity issues? Which parts do you find yourself losing interest in? The rough cut is for content, not technical quality, so you can ignore slightly dodgy edits right now.

Now you've got your rough cut, and you know how long it is when you have just made edits for content. You may have a target time for your interview, for example, a common duration for a podcast to aim for is 25 minutes, to fit into most people's commute, so you know how much more you need to cut.

The second cut

Now you know your rough cut duration, you can start looking for extra cuts to make. Depending on how you did your rough cut, this might be removing filler words, such as "um" and "like", chopping out repetitions and stutters and generally just cleaning up the interview. I tend to do this starting from the beginning of the interview and working my way through chronologically, unlike the first cut which was done from the paper edit and so had to work backwards.

By the time you've finished with your second cut, you should have the interview down to the duration you're aiming for, so that you can start doing your finer edits.

If you are working with other people, there will likely be a third or even fourth cut that are just different variations of the second cut.

The final cut

Once you've bashed your interview into rough shape, it's time to take out a finer chisel and go over the cuts to finesse them down to something natural sounding. When you get good at editing, nobody will be able to tell where you've made the cuts. This is done last so that you don't waste a bunch of time and effort making really neat edits that just get chopped out later anyway.

Now you can drag it over to your master episode session.

Mixing

Mixing is the art of balancing all the audio in a project, making sure it all sits nicely with perfect fades, pleasantly levelled music and clear speech, which is why some people call it balancing. This is a whole process in itself, which is why an entire section of this book is on mixing!

You can do some initial mixing during your final cut if you prefer, but a podcast should be balanced across the entire episode, so this stage is best left until everything is sitting in one project.

Mastering

Mastering can mean a bunch of different things to different people, but essentially this is creating your master copy. This is turning your multi-track project into a single WAV or MP3 ready to publish.

You can apply processing or do some final edits to this master file, if you think it needs it.

Tip: add 0.5 seconds of silence to the start and end of your file to ensure it plays properly in all apps. Some podcast playing apps clip the start a little and it can sound jumpy without some silence added.

Editing speech, naturally

You can do a rough cut with even the most basic editing skills. It is the finer edits and the ability to make them sound totally natural that really separates the professional podcast editors from the amateurs.

Making speech edits sound natural is a real skill. You have to listen critically, experiment and try out different cuts to see what works.

Human speech is full of subtle cues that tell our brain what the speaker is going to do next, so when you're editing you shouldn't just be thinking about what a person is saying, but also how they are saying it. An interview edit that doesn't take these cues into account will sound unnatural and jarring to a listener.

You generally don't want your interview to sound like it has been edited, at least to the untrained ear. You do want to make your interview sound natural and your speakers to sound like great conversationalists. Cut out the unnecessary filler and boring stuff... but make it sound like they were just that interesting to begin with.

Before we get started on the actual process of making an edit, there are some guiding principles to think about when you make an edit.

Edit with your ears

This might seem obvious, but make sure you listen a lot:

- Listen to the speaker's natural, unedited cadence. This is what you are trying to mimic.
- Listen to every edit you make, including a few seconds before it.
- Listen back to the whole edit when you've finished.

Your listeners aren't going to be looking at the multitrack session; they're only going to hear the edited interview. Try looking away from your screen after you've made an edit to judge whether it sounds natural when you can't see the cuts yourself.

Always listen on headphones. Even if you don't do most of your editing and mixing on headphones, the majority of your listeners will be listening on headphones. Headphones provide a different kind of intimacy to a car stereo, kitchen radio or speakers – they are particularly unforgiving to choppy edits and harsh mixing. The audio is being pumped directly to a listener's eardrum, so you need to get that experience of your own show too.

Intonation is key

When someone is ending a sentence their speech will lower in pitch, giving it a sense of finality. Similarly, if they intend to continue talking, their intonation will either stay flat or perhaps rise a little.

Picture someone saying this sentence aloud:

So, I said to him, I am going outside.

It is broken up into three parts:

- "So,
- I said to him,
- I am going outside".

You hear the upward inflection in the first two parts followed by the final, downward inflection on the "I am going outside".

"You're going outside?" is a question, and demands an answer with the rising inflection at the end. More speech is expected.

So intonation is really important in speech, and when we are editing audio we need to listen carefully for intonation and make sure we make our edits on the appropriate inflections, otherwise it will sound unnatural and jarring to the listener.

- If you are chopping off the end of a sentence, creating a new end, make sure it ends on a downward inflection.
- When cutting out the middle of a sentence, aim for a flat or upward inflection, although this is less important and can still sound natural provided you have the appropriate pause after a downward inflection.

Making edits when the intonation is wrong is a very common mistake, but it's very easily avoided.

Pacing

People naturally speed up and slow down when they are speaking. Sometimes they are excited and their speech becomes quicker, more breathless. Sometimes they become more thoughtful and slow down, taking longer pauses to consider what they are saying.

Make sure you reflect this when you are editing. Don't assume that the length of pause between sentences that worked in one segment will also work in another.

Similarly, it can be easy to see lots of gaps and think that an easy way to cut your interview's duration down is to shorten them, but these can be important to the pacing of the interview

Breaths

Generally breaths are your friend when you are editing. They're pretty interchangeable and can be crossfaded over easily. Avoid leaving a large gap between a breath and the start of a word though, this can sound unnatural.

A good technique for having a natural sounding gap between a breath and a word is to cut before the breath and use the breath that went with that word anyway – nothing is going to be more natural than the actual gap left by the speaker (Figure 4.3)!

Use your wildtrack

When you need to bring two sentences together that feel like they need a little bit of a pause, grab that wildtrack we told you to record earlier and fade it in and out under the edit. A listener's ears would subconsciously notice that little silence even if they didn't realise it and the edit would become obvious… so cover it (Figure 4.4)!

Get rid of the gross stuff

Your edit should sound natural, but not… too natural. Nobody wants to hear your guest's lips smacking or snotty sniffles. Cut this right out.

Crossfade

You should always start and end audio clips with a fade, even if it is just a few milliseconds. A lot of DAWs will do this automatically for you, but if you are using one that doesn't, it can create a popping sound. This is caused by a wave form not starting at zero (Figure 4.5).

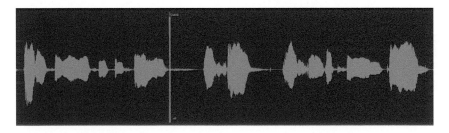

Figure 4.3 Breath cut.

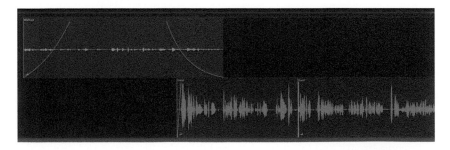

Figure 4.4 Wildtrack use.

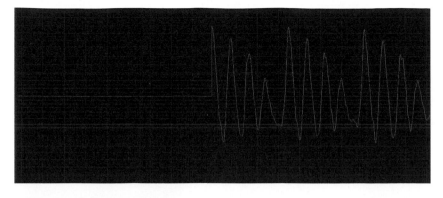

Figure 4.5 Non-zero crossing.

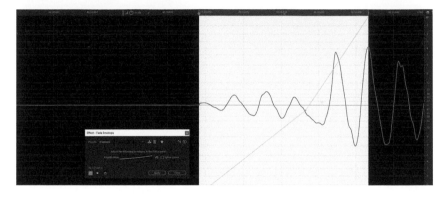

Figure 4.6 Fade curve.

Audition does compensate for popping, but to do your own fades it is really easy: using the move tool, click in the top left or right corner of a clip and drag to create the fade in or out, respectively. You can also drag up or down to change the curve of the fade (Figure 4.6).

That curve represents the volume of the clip, with it reaching full volume when the line is at the top of the clip.

The process is exactly the same in Pro-Tools, although the move tool is called the "smart tool".

A crossfade is where two pieces of audio overlap, one fades out as the other fades in. This is an important tool for editing speech. Most of your edits should be crossfaded so that any ambient noise of the room doesn't drop out, which would give the listener a subtle cue that an edit has been made.

Adobe Audition will make a crossfade for you if you drag two pieces of audio over each other. You can then use the move tool to adjust the curve and duration of the fade (Figure 4.7).

Be mindful of the gaps between words here, and use your wildtrack to create an artificial space if necessary.

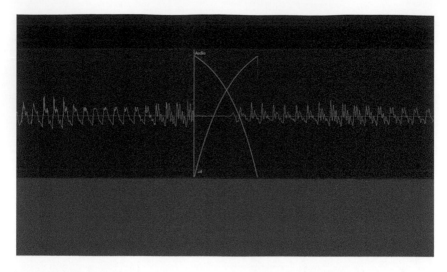

Figure 4.7 Crossfade.

If you recorded in a professional studio or just somewhere with very low ambient noise, then you might get away with a few more gaps without wildtrack and just regular fades.

Not all gaps are bad

Often you have a target duration to hit for an interview and the instinct is to cut down all long pauses… but think about each one. Sometimes that pregnant pause while a speaker collects their thoughts can say just as much as the sentence that comes after it.

You should try and match any gaps you introduce with your edits to the natural pace and cadence of your speaker. If they rush along without pausing for breath, then try shorter gaps and vice versa if they are a more considered, slow speaker.

OK, let's actually make a cut

For every podcast you edit, you will repeat this process countless times.

Here is a piece of audio in Adobe Audition's multitrack view. The speaker has said, "This is an example piece of audio, which I am recording to be used as an example, I hope someone will make me sound like I know what I am talking about" (Figure 4.8).

We want to remove the middle chunk of that sentence: "… which I am recording to be used as an example", so that there is no repetition:

1   Switch to the razor tool and listen until we find the start of the cut.
2   Zoom in and make a cut with the razor right before the word starts.

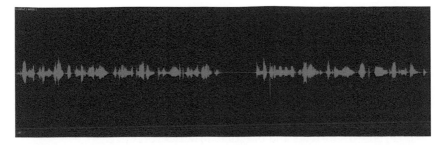

Figure 4.8 Unedited example.

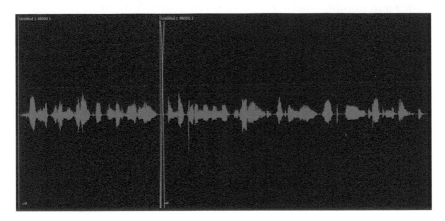

Figure 4.9 Edited example.

3 Find the end of the passage and make another cut. You don't want to double up on pauses, so make the cut *before the start of the first word of the next passage.* Leave just enough of a pause to crossfade the ambient sound (Figure 4.9).
4 Select the passage to be deleted with your move tool and hit delete.
5 Select everything to the right of the gap (hopefully you have set a key command for this!) and using the move tool drag it back to close the gap.
6 Listen to the edit.
7 Make smaller adjustments to the position and crossfade to make it sound natural.
8 Listen again!

This process is the thing you will do the most of when you edit speech, so you will get a lot of practice.

As you practice more the editing process will get quicker and quicker, and eventually you'll be making edits like this in a few seconds.

In Adobe Audition you can also use the time selection tool to select the area you want to delete. This allows you to preview the edit before you've made it by having "skip selection" selected.

Use the time markers at the top of your screen to fine-tune your selection, then use ripple delete (usually assigned to ctrl + shift + backspace) to make the cut.

Ultimately, you might find some variation of both of these that is more efficient for the way you edit. DAWs are flexible pieces of software with many ways to achieve a result, these are just two. Experiment, set your own keyboard shortcuts and practice, practice, practice.

Fades and automation

Fading in and out of audio clips is a really key part of learning to edit audio, so let's get a little more detailed.

A fade is, as you probably know, a gradual increase or decrease in volume.

On a technical level, you need at least a small fade in and out of every piece of audio you place in the multitrack timeline, otherwise you are likely to get pops on your finished product as the signal starts at a position other than zero.

From a creative point of view, it also just sounds much more natural to have atmospheric sound fade in rather than just cut in suddenly.

In Adobe Audition and Pro-Tools you can create a basic fade by clicking the top corner of a clip in the multitrack window and dragging into the clip to set the duration. This will create a linear fade.

Types of fades

Linear fade

This is the most basic type of fade (Figure 4.10).

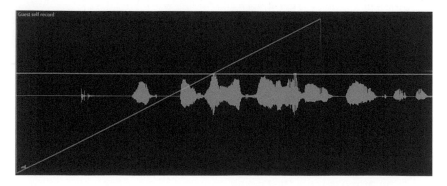

Figure 4.10 Linear fade.

The volume curve is a straight line. Because of the way our ears perceive sound, this doesn't sound like a particularly natural fade. In fact, despite being a straight line, it actually sounds like the fade speeds up as it goes. This is because our ears perceive volume in a logarithmic way.

Don't write the linear fade off though – sometimes you want an unnatural sounding fade as a creative technique or sometimes the goal is just to avoid a pop, so a quick, short linear fade will do the job.

Logarithmic fade

A logarithmic fade is curved, and because we perceive sound in a logarithmic way it sounds much more natural than a linear fade (Figure 4.11).

With a fade in, the fade gets quicker as it goes on. When fading out, the fade starts quick and becomes slower. You can see this represented in the shape of the curve.

You can create these in Adobe Audition and Pro-Tools the same way as a linear fade, but drag up or down as well as left or right.

Exponential

An exponential curve is basically an upside-down logarithmic curve. Generally, this is more of a tool than a creative effect that is used to bring audio in quickly without a hard cut in (Figure 4.12).

These are really useful for editing speech when you just need a sentence to be cut in or out naturally without it sounding like a slow fade.

It's worth noting here that in most cases, "exponential" and "logarithmic" mean almost, if not exactly the same thing. This is just how most audio producers refer to these styles of fade when producing.

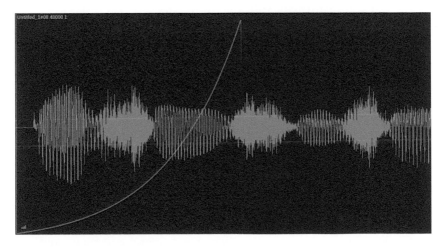

Figure 4.11 Logarithmic fade.

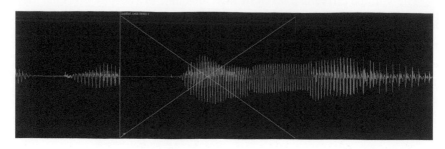

Figure 4.12 Exponential fade.

Fading with atmospheric sound

Short and long

CROSSFADES

Crossfade just means fading from one piece of audio to another as opposed to fading to/from silence. In Adobe Audition and Pro-Tools you can do this on the same track, but two separately programmed fades on two separate tracks also counts as a crossfade. It's all about how it sounds when you're done, after all.

The crossfade is super useful when editing anything with a degree of background noise. You should always crossfade your background noise to make sure that it doesn't suddenly change or drop out between sentences in speech, making the edit obvious.

As covered in the previous chapter, you can create a crossfade by dragging two pieces of audio over each other and Audition will create a fade which you can then tweak with the move tool. Pro-Tools has a similar feature if you overlap the audio and hit ctrl + f.

Equal power or equal gain?

Similar to a single fade, crossfades can be linear or logarithmic. Equal gain is the crossfade version of a linear fade, with the two clips fading in and out at the same linear rate (Figure 4.13).

As the human ear doesn't perceive sound levels in a linear way, this creates the effect of a dip in loudness around the midpoint. That's great for a creative effect – when you want one piece of audio to fade into another totally different piece. The dip in volume creates a good subconscious midpoint at which the second piece of audio becomes dominant.

It's not as useful however if you are crossfading between two pieces of background noise in an interview edit and just want a seamless transition. The dip would show that there has been an edit made and can disrupt the flow of the interview. That's why you need an equal power crossfade (Figure 4.14).

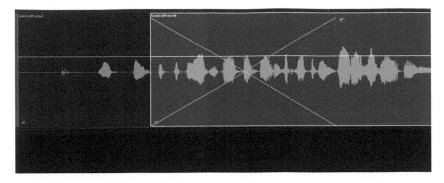

Figure 4.13 Equal gain.

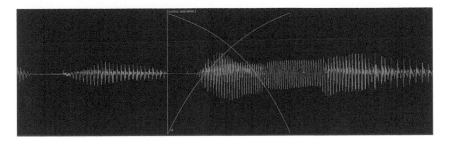

Figure 4.14 Equal power.

Equal power makes the midpoint a little higher in volume to compensate for the loss in perceived loudness. Audition does this automatically when you first drag the clips across each other, so you have to tweak the fade if you do want a linear fade (it will snap to the linear midpoint when you drag it down).

Linear or cosine?

If you right click on the fade button in Audition, you also see the option to choose between linear and cosine. There are mathematical equations behind how the shape of the cosine is calculated, but for making podcasts they aren't really relevant; all you need to know is that it changes the shape of the fade curve to be a little more like what you would experience in natural sound.

Automation

A fade is a really powerful tool. The methods we've already been over are powerful ways of creating beautiful fades that sound natural or musical, but often we need a lot more control over volume over longer periods. This is where automation comes in.

Automation is one of the things that you need to get really comfortable with. It's the tool that will turn you from a good podcast editor to a great one, so pay close attention to this section and spend some time practicing.

Automation, at its core is a set of instructions that tell your software to do certain things at certain time codes. The most common automation that we will use in podcast production is volume, so that instruction might be "adjust volume to −10dBFS". Usually, your automation will consist of a bunch of these instructions in sequence.

In Audition the automation instructions are called keyframes – a hangover from video production. The term automation is itself something of a hangover as it refers to a physical mixing desks having motors built into them to reduce the need for multiple operators.

By default, volume automation is visible on clips in Adobe Audition and is represented by the yellow line on the clip in the multitrack. The clip shown below has some automation already programmed in.

Each of the dots on this line are keyframes. You create them by double clicking on the line, modify them by dragging them around and delete them by either dragging them off the clip or right clicking and selecting "delete selected keyframes" (Figure 4.15).

If you don't see this line, click "View" in the toolbar at the top of Audition and then "Show Clip Volume Envelopes".

In Pro-Tools you have to click the track view selector to the left of your track and change it from "waveform" to "volume", which will bring up the volume line.

You will use volume automation a lot. It's a very common way of balancing audio in podcasts, both to bring speech within loudness standards and for creative balancing of different elements like music, speech and wildtrack.

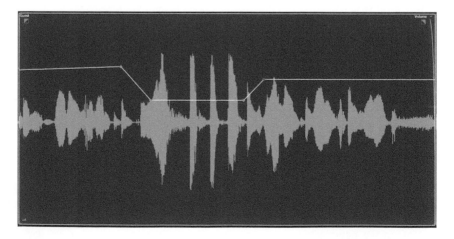

Figure 4.15 Automation.

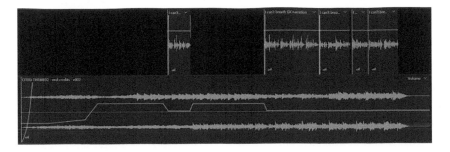

Figure 4.16 Music automation.

For example, you might want to bring in some music to establish the theme, then dip it back down to allow the voice-over to cut through and take dominance in the mix, before bringing the music back up to punctuate the voice-over. That would look a little like this (Figure 4.16):

When working with volume automation, 0 deciBels (dB) should be your starting point that the line returns to. There's a whole separate chapter to this book on mixing where we will get into much more detail, but your overall balance shouldn't be achieved with automation. Automation is for creative effects and smoothing out audio that differs in volume over time.

Balancing speech

Speech has natural variations in volume. There are a number of ways that podcast editors compensate for this, but automation is one of the best ways to keep speech at an even level while maintaining the natural sounding dynamics. Most producers refer to this as levelling.

The end goal when levelling is for the listener not to have to change the volume while they listen. There also shouldn't be any sudden jumps in volume, which can be jarring or even painful when listening on headphones.

You're also avoiding the clipping that can be caused by peaks.

Podcasts differ from levelling for TV or radio, in that the vast majority of listeners do listen on headphones, so you have to keep in mind that you are pumping sound directly into a listener's ears.

Compressors are great for bring down peaks, but if you rely on them for doing all your speech levelling, it will sound unnatural and quite harsh, especially when listening on headphones, so it pays dividends to spend some time going over the speech doing finer, segmented volume automation (Figure 4.17).

To keep the speech sounding natural, these automation changes should be kept relatively macro, as in the example above. Bring up periods where the speaker has naturally gotten quieter and bringing down periods where they have gotten much quieter, perhaps running out of breath. Try to keep these changes in volume less than –6dB, and gradual over at least

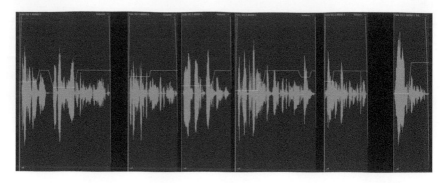

Figure 4.17 Speech automation.

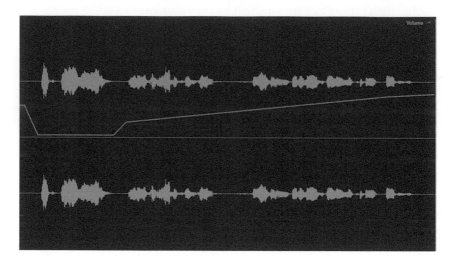

Figure 4.18 Speech automation (slow fade).

half a second. You can do that gradual change between words too; just avoid a sudden jump in volume as even a tiny bit of atmospheric sound on the mic track will be noticeable if it suddenly changes intensity.

You can see here an example of a very gradual shift in volume to compensate for a speaker who starts their sentences loudly and then gets noticeably quieter as they continue (Figure 4.18).

Speech also often contains sudden, large peaks. Once you get to the mixing stage, using a compressor to catch these is one way of tackling big peaks; however, this can also sound unnatural.

Laughing is a really good example of something that benefits from maintaining a natural dynamic but is also a difficult large peak, so you want to bring the whole laugh down rather than have a compressor just catch the peaks.

Levelling is really as much an art as a science. Yes, we are aiming for a specific loudness reading of –16LUFS, but you should also be listening and using your ears to make judgements.

LUFS, by the way, is one of the ways we measure "loudness". You can read all about that in Chapter 5.

Using automation to place music, effects and wildtrack underneath speech

As always, use your ears to work out what sounds best and play around until you get a good sounding edit; however, there are a few good places to start.

When fading music or other audio underneath speech, make sure the fade starts a little before the speech so that the listener gets a subtle cue that something else is about to happen and the music's volume is already low enough for the speech to take dominance by the time it comes in. Try a second to begin with and make it longer or shorter depending on the pacing of your show.

Where your music comes to rest underneath the speech is definitely a matter of aural judgement, but between –14dbFS and –20dbFS is generally a good range to be in (Figure 4.19).

When bringing music up at the end of speech, you should also try fading it up slightly before the speech ends; however, don't take it to full volume until the speech has ended. This gives the listener a subtle cue that the speech segment is ending without allowing the speech to get lost in the music.

Wildtrack is ambient atmospheric sound, and as such it shouldn't have artificial sounding boosts in volume around the speech. Fade the wildtrack in with a nice, creative slow sweep – probably a logarithmic fade – and then keep it at one level. If you are using automation throughout the wildtrack, then it should be to compensate for natural changes in volume in the atmospheric sound.

Other uses for automation

Automation isn't just for volume. It can be applied to pretty much any parameter in your DAW. Pan (moving audio from left to right) is easily

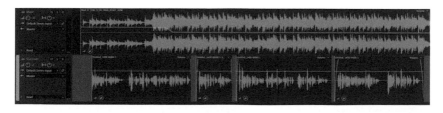

Figure 4.19 Music and speech automation.

available in Adobe Audition – you just click View > Show Clip Pan Envelopes and a blue line appears on your clips.

For most other forms of automation, you need to prep your DAW to
read the automation track for that parameter. In Audition there is a setting on the track controls that by default is set to "read". For podcast
production, you should probably leave it on this. This lets you draw your
automation points on with your mouse and then play it back.

It can also be set to "write", which allows you to manually create automation points in real time using a hardware controller such as a mixing
desk. Latch and touch are similar to write, but latch will allow you to
play back previously written automation points until you first change a
parameter, and from that point it will keep writing. Touch is the same as
latch, but with gradual returns settings to previously written or default
values when you stop changing them.

Let's assume that you're drawing automation manually with your
mouse though.

Reverb tails

A cool creative use of automation is with reverb. You can take a sound
from completely dry to really echoey to create the effect of it getting more
distant. You can use this to bring something else into clear focus in comparison or for a dramatic creative end to something. You could also draw
out the end of a piece of music with extra reverb.

To do this, add your chosen reverb effect to the track's effect rack
(Figure 4.20).

Now we need to let our DAW know that we are automating the "Wet"
parameter. In audio effects there is a dry level and a wet level. Dry is the
original, clean sound without any effect on it. Wet is the processed sound.

In Audition we do this by clicking the small arrow next to where we set
automation to "read", click "show envelopes" and select the parameter
we want to automate. A new set of lines will appear underneath the audio
track.

Bear in mind that unlike the volume and pan automation which
appears on the audio clips in the multitrack, these automation points are
locked to the *track*'s time code, not to the clip's, so if you make a bunch
of edits that change where the clip is, then your automation is going to be
in the wrong place. For that reason it's best to do this after all your other
edits are done, so you don't have to redo it all.

This sound here is completely dry. To create this effect, you want to
take the wet level from 0% to 100% (Figure 4.21).

If you want to accentuate the affect, you can also automate the dry
level down at the same time (Figure 4.22).

Try this out instead of a crossfade between two pieces of music... or
perhaps on some old archive newsreel to get an effective transition.

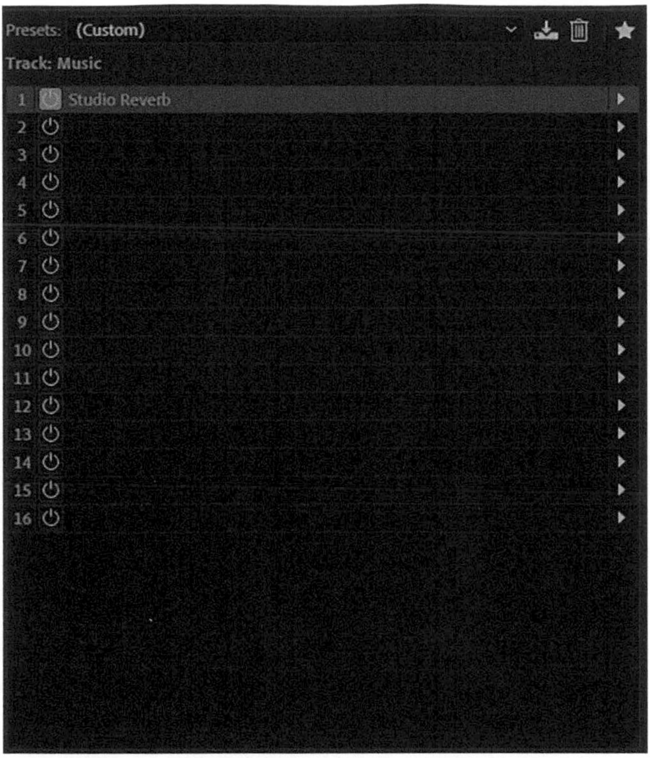

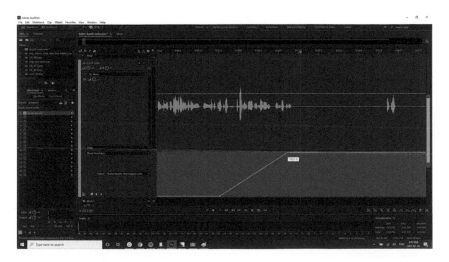

Figure 4.20 Reverb on effects rack.

Figure 4.21 Reverb wet auto.

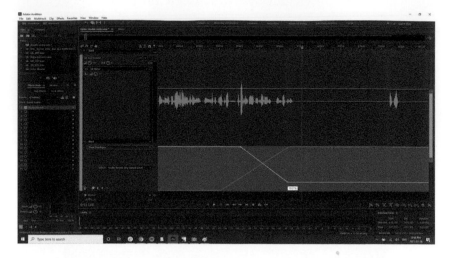

Figure 4.22 Reverb wet and dry auto.

EQ automation

The equaliser (EQ) is a powerful corrective tool, but one of the most fun ways to use it is with some creative automation. If you automate the frequency of a low pass and start it at 20,000hz, that is, at the top of the range of human hearing, and bring it right down to around 100hz, you can effectively fade your audio out in a different sounding way to a volume fade. Think of the effect of slowly closing the door from a noisy concert – muffling it slowly. It's called a filter sweep and it is another cool way to crossfade between things, fade out audio or just create interesting effects.

You can also try a similar effect from the opposite direction, using a high pass filter and sweeping up from 20hz to 20,000hz. Try turning the "Q" setting up on your EQ to create a more noticeable sweep.

Once you've got comfortable with volume automation and tried out these two techniques, you'll see that automation is a really powerful tool. It can be applied to any parameter on any effect, and making effective use of it is one of the things that separates a great podcast producer from a mediocre one.

Using field effects and archive audio

Even if you are just making a simple conversation or interview format podcast, you can find ways to include outside audio to liven things up and provide some illustration.

For example, say you are editing an interview with someone who is talking about when they were speaking at a protest – did anyone record the speech? Is their news footage of people chanting at the protest? Rights permitting, you could break up the interview with some of that audio.

Think of when you watch TV news. The director doesn't just cut between the reporter and the host – they run footage of what the reporter is talking about, either over the top or in a box to the side. We can do something similar with audio, although the technique is different.

With pretty much all of these, you should be taking note of whether they are in stereo or mono – make sure that you put them on the right kind of track in your DAW or you might run into phase issues.

Intelligibility is really important to remember when using audio that is from outside the studio. You're far more likely to encounter problems with recordings when not in that controlled environment or when using audio you haven't sourced yourself. **If you have to listen to it more than once to understand it, then you shouldn't use it**. Well, maybe you should, we'll cover that in a bit.

Ways to increase intelligibility

You can clear up some difficult to understand speech by boosting useful frequencies and removing some unhelpful ones. Jump over the EQ section of the mixing chapter if you need some help here:

- Key frequencies for understanding speech are between 2,000Hz and 4,000Hz, so if your audio is just a little unclear try adding a bit of a boost around this area in the EQ.
- From 200Hz to 500Hz is the muddiest part of the frequency spectrum; try cutting here a little.
- Try cutting out the low end entirely with a high pass filter in the EQ set to around 200Hz. A lot of useless rumble can happen in this part of the spectrum and cutting it out gives you more headroom to boost the rest of the audio.

Actuality

Actuality is a fancy radio way of saying "the sound of something happening". This could be newsreel or the sound of you knocking on an interviewee's door and introducing yourself. Maybe it's the sound of a busy street you walked through on the way to interview someone, which you are using to set the scene.

As with field effects, the transitions from voice-over to actuality are the difference between something sounding polished.

You might find it harder to make internal edits that aren't noticeable – a longer crossfade can help here.

Field Recordings are one type of actuality and will almost definitely have noticeable background noise; in fact, it might be the background noise that you want. Because of this, you should include a nice long sweep of a fade when you bring it in. You might want to tuck this under the voice-over if the voice-over is talking about something related to what's about to happen. If you're changing scene entirely, you could start from cold.

Archive audio

Sometimes you'll be working with an old scratchy audio pulled from radio in the 1970s. There's loads of it available free online, and it does sound kind of cool.

These old recordings are inevitably low fidelity, perhaps even slightly difficult to understand. That's part of the charm of the audio, of course, but you do need to understand what you're working with and how to make it a little clearer.

The audio is often lacking in top end, leading it to sound quite muffled. Now you can't add in frequencies that don't exist (and it is unlikely that there is going to be much over 5,000Hz), but you can boost the range that the human ear finds most useful. Use some EQ to add a boost around the 2,000Hz–2,400Hz range. If you need help on this, check out the EQ section of the chapter on mixing.

Having often already been through a broadcast chain, these recordings are likely to be quite compressed, so make sure you aren't adding more compression in your own chain. This compression makes the perceived loudness higher than your voice-over and other uncompressed files, so adjust the volume accordingly.

Your instinct might be to try cleaning it up with some noise reduction software... don't. The scratchiness is a good signifier to the listener that they are listening to something old, and it's probably past the point of being reparable anyway.

Talk tape

Intelligibility is really important. Usually, there isn't much point including something if your listener can't understand it; however, there are occasions where you have really important audio that you want to include, despite it not being entirely clear what is happening from the audio alone. In these situations you can use a technique called "Talk Tape". This is where you run the tape but have your host voice-over the top of it explaining what's happening.

It's important to make sure the listener still hears plenty of the actual audio, unclear as it may be. Run a few seconds to establish it, dip it down with volume automation and have the host voice-over explain what's going on.

If you find that your voice-over doesn't fit exactly around where you want to bring your audio up – the parts you want to highlight – you can cheat.

Cut the audio a few times so that you have the parts you want to highlight in separate clips and place it around the voice-over.

Now extend the non-voice-over audio underneath the voice-over from both sides, creating a crossfade underneath the voice-over. Make sure it's actually a part where the voice-over is speaking so that it covers the crossfade. With your volume automation programmed in, the listener shouldn't notice the edit.

You can use this on recordings that are important to the story but difficult to understand. A good example of that would be a really great interview you got with someone who was at the event you are making a documentary about... but you can only reach them on a really poor quality phone line.

Alternatively, if an interviewee is important to the story in your documentary but not the most engaging speaker, you can use this technique to summarise what they are saying.

You can even use it as an alternative to translating in full an interview done in a language other than your podcast's.

Tips to get you out of a difficult cut

Occasionally there is an edit you really want to make, but the inflections don't work or the timing of breaths is difficult. Perhaps pulling a whole question and answer (Q&A) segment out makes the interview feel like it takes a sharp turn, or perhaps it's just a bunch of stuttering and "ums", "aahs" and "likes" that you want to take out because they make it a difficult listen.

Once you have perfected the basic editing covered in this chapter, you can start trying out some more advanced edits. You'll start to recognise what different sounds look like in the waveform representing your speech audio, and you can work with those to do some really tricky work.

Sibilants and breaths

Sibilants is just the fancy way of saying the "sssss" sounds.

Here's a little secret: sibilants are basically just little bursts of high frequency noise. The brain can't really tell the difference between one sibilant and another. It's impossible to add an inflection to a sibilant sound, upwards or downwards. This makes them very useful for editing, so if someone stutters on a word with a sibilant sound... you can crossfade between the two really easily.

They tend to look a little like this in the edit (Figure 4.23):

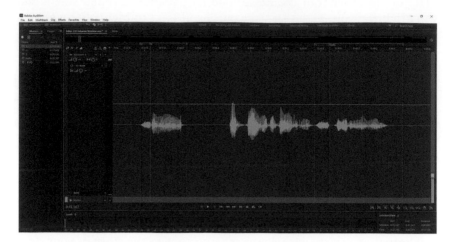

Figure 4.23 Sibilants in audition.

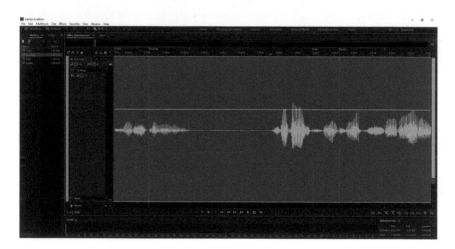

Figure 4.24 Hard sounds in audition.

So if, um like, someone says "uh", say that someone says a sentence like this one written here, you could easily crossfade between that first "so" and the "say that" to create a stutter-free sentence.

Transients

First part of a hard consonant such as a "p", "b" or "d" is also free of inflection and stands alone from the rest of the word in the waveform, once again making it pretty easy to move about (Figure 4.24).

In the example above you can see the "T" sounds in "contracts" and "constraining". You should also now be able to identify the sibilant sounds in both those words.

Using hard sounds as edit points can quite easily join the first part of a speaker stumbling over a word and the final part of a completed word to create a whole word without a listener noticing the edit.

Music

Sometimes no matter what you do, two sections of an interview just won't edit together without sounding like a sharp change in tone. To avoid something that jarring, a common technique is to fade in some music that indicates a change in mood.

Create a short musical bridge to the next section. Often using the very end of a piece of music creates a satisfying feeling of punctuation.

Advanced intonation magic

There are sneaky ways to alter the inflection at the end of a speaker once you have gotten more confident at audio editing and are experimenting with more plug-ins. You can use the pitch shifting tool in Adobe Audition called "Pitch Bender" to bend the pitch of the audio, similar to how you would with automation. You have to do this destructively in the waveform edit window, so make sure you keep a backup of your original audio:

*   Set the pitch range low, only around 2–5 semitones, depending on the natural range of the speaker.
*   Have the last words pitched down slightly. Subtle changes can make a lot of difference here.
*   Don't get too drastic as the change in pitch will sound unnatural.

It's tough to get right, but if you have the time to play around this can get you out of a bind.

Izotope makes a plug-in called Dialogue Contour that is designed exactly for this purpose and makes it much easier to fix off-key intonation; however, it's part of the $1000 RX 8 package, so only available to those with some extra software budget.

Exercise: remote recording, part 2

Let's get back to learning how to record remotely and turn that into a multitrack edit session.

If you haven't done the first exercise yet, skip back and try that out. Being on the location end of a tape sync is often the first step into professional podcast production, especially if you don't live in one of the major production hub cities.

In this exercise we are going to see what it is like on the other end of the remote recording. You are going to be the interviewer and you are going to talk your guest through recording themselves into their smartphone. You're also going to record yourself at your end.

Recording your remote interview

- Enlist the help of a friend, family member or fellow student. The less technically minded your "guest" is, the better.
- Read Chapter 3, "Remote Recording and Double Enders", and then talk your "guest" through recording themselves into their smartphone.
- Connect to them over Zoom, Skype or however you'd prefer to communicate.
- Conduct a mock interview with your guest, record yourself and pay attention to how they use their phone to record. Try and get the best audio possible. The edit will be easier if you hit record at the same time you tell your guest to press record.
- Once you're done, have them stop the recording and send the audio over.

By the time you are done, you should have two pieces of audio:

1   The location recording
2   The Interviewer's recording

Now it's up to a producer to do the "sync" part.

Part 1: sync

1   Create a multitrack session in your DAW of choice.
2   Create two new mono channels.
3   If the recordings aren't already mono WAV files, convert them.
4   Drag your own recorded audio on to track 1 and the guest's on to track 2.
5   Line the clips up on their individual tracks, so everything is in the order that happened during the recording.
6   Group the clips together (Ctrl + G in Audition)
7   Trim the start and end so that your clips are exactly the same length and you've removed all the extraneous audio on either side.

Congratulations – your tape is synced! Now you're ready to start an edit.
   You might notice that no matter how hard you try to line up the two recordings, there is some drift as the interview progresses. This is unavoidable and is due to slight variations in hardware and software between different computers and pieces of equipment. In professional studios,

recordings are kept synced together by a "master clock". You just have to fix this as you go through the edit.

Listen back to this synced up audio and try and identify issues with the remote recording.

COMMON PROBLEMS

- The recording suddenly stops early: the guest didn't place their phone in airplane mode and received a call.
- Clipping/distorted audio: the guest is holding their phone directly in front of their mouth instead of to their ear.
- Mid-to-high-pitched "slithering" or clicking sounds: the guest is touching or handling their headset cable.
- Large amounts of echo: the guest chose a space with too many reflective surfaces and/or held the phone too far away.
- Constant humming noises: the guest hasn't turned off appliances like air conditioning.

Now, repeat this exercise with the audio you recorded in exercise 1. Listen and compare the two sets of audio.

Part 2: edit

In this part of the exercise your goal is to get your audio down to half its original length while still having the interview make sense. Use the skills you learned in this chapter and chop out the parts you don't find interesting as well as unnecessary mouth noises.

Have the interview start clean on a question and end on the end of an answer.

By the end you should have something that sounds like an engaging conversation, free of interruptions and gross stuff.

If you want to get creative, try adding in some music at the beginning and end of the interview.

Now, do the same with the other multitrack session so that you have two edited interviews, ready to be mixed.

Save both of these sessions and the associated audio, we're going to come back to them in Exercise 3.

5   Mixing

Introduction to mixing

Once you've edited all your audio into place in the multitrack, it is time to start mixing. You've got a rough assembly that tells the story but the levels are all over the place and some parts are difficult to hear. That's why we mix.

Mixing is the art and science of balancing all your audio in a way that sounds pleasant, doesn't require additional effort from the listener and adheres to industry standards.

While mixing is an art, there are still very clear goals when mixing a podcast:

- The listener can hear everything clearly, without having to go back and check again
- The listener doesn't need to adjust their volume control throughout the show
- The mix isn't harsh to listen to over an extended period
- The show meets industry loudness standards

Being the audio engineer who does the final mix is a coveted position in film and music. People spend their careers working up to it. In podcasting that responsibility often falls directly on you, the producer... and you might be the show host too, so it's OK to feel a little intimidated by this process. You're learning.

Basics: pan, gain, volume

The signal chain

Before we start mixing, we need to understand that your audio goes through a chain. There are often volume controls at each stage of this chain which also provides a risk of causing clipping at each stage, so we need to know where we are amplifying the signal at each stage (Figure 5.1). Your effects processing like equaliser (EQ), compression and reverb might go before or after the volume fader. This is controlled with the

DOI: 10.4324/9781003046578-5

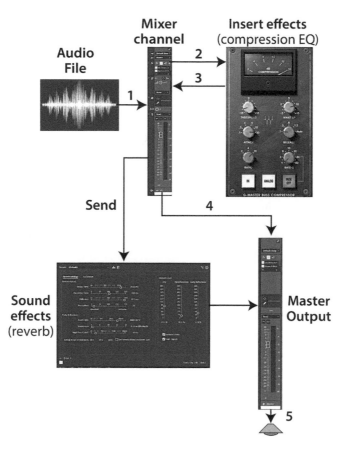

Figure 5.1 Signal chain.

"pre-fader/post-fader" settings on the mixer. For spacial effects like reverb, they might be on a separate branch of the signal chain called a "bus", which is achieved through sending a duplicate of your audio through a "send".

Let's get started with that all important levelling. We have kind of covered a lot of different parts of the process of getting all your audio balanced so it might feel like we are covering some of the same ground here, but it was all in preparation for that all important balance.

Volume and gain controls

The first stage of mixing is to work out what is too loud and too quiet *overall*. This means listening and watching the level metres and setting the overall volume for that entire track.

If you are wondering about the difference between volume and gain, well I can't blame you, they are similar concepts.

Gain is applied on the channel input and amplifies or cuts the incoming signal. Volume is applied on channel output. Once your audio is recorded and in your Digital Audio Workstation (DAW), there won't be many places you apply true gain.

Most DAWs have a "mixer", with virtual volume faders that allow you to set the overall volume for a whole track (Figure 5.2).

Audition also has controls on the multitrack view – these do the same as the faders.

In fact, most DAWs have quite a lot of different points at which you can boost or cut your overall signal. If you look in the picture above as well as the controls by the track, you can see that the effects rack has an "input" and "output" volume control. You could just as easily use these to set your overall track level, and some people prefer this as it means they can turn off that adjustment when they turn the effects rack off.

Regardless, pay attention to the volume metres, measured in deciBels (dB), and make sure your audio signal isn't hitting the red at any stage in the signal chain.

Pan

Most podcasts are in stereo, meaning there are two channels: left and right. The pan control determines how much of a mono signal is sent to the left or right. If it is set to zero, the centre, then equal amounts are sent to each channel and the listener will perceive it as being in the centre of

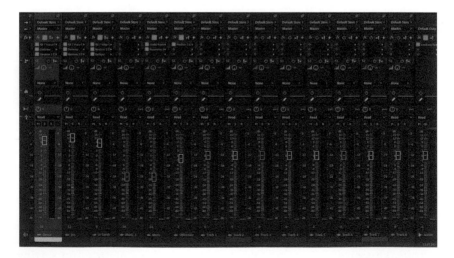

Figure 5.2 Mixer.

the stereo field. Turn the control to the left and you'll increase the volume in the left channel while decreasing it in the right channel, causing the listener to perceive the audio on the left of the stereo field.

To compensate for signals appearing louder in the centre than when panned to the left or right, most DAWs apply "pan law", a 3dB attenuation of the signal when it is in the centre. That shouldn't really affect how you mix your show but it's useful to know.

Your podcast will probably be released in stereo, doing otherwise would lead to phase issues in stereo signals like music. Despite this, you should still mix under the assumption that someone somewhere will be listening in mono, because someone somewhere probably will – whether that is just having one ear of their headphones in or playing through a smart speaker.

That means not panning things your listener needs to hear too extremely. Pan is rarely used in podcast production with most voices being kept in the centre of the stereo field; however, it can be useful if you have two people with similar voices to subtly move one to the left and another to the right. By subtle, we mean no more than 15%.

Loudness and levels

Loudness

Loudness is a very untechnical sounding word for a very technical part of podcast production. It refers to the subjective perception of sound pressure – literally how loud something seems.

This chapter on mixing starts with loudness because it is so important. The goal, when mixing a show, is to have all your audio properly balanced at the right loudness.

We're aiming for the right loudness so that your show doesn't sound quiet in comparison to other podcasts and music. A lot of people listen to podcasts on their phones, for example. Most smartphones don't turn up particularly loud, so if your show is noticeably quieter than everything else they listen to they are going to get annoyed and skip it. It also helps us be consistent across multiple episodes.

Imagine you are in your car or maybe on the bus listening to your favourite show and you get a recommendation from Spotify to try out a new show. You hit play and there is a big drop in volume. You already had your headphones turned up pretty loud but you crank them up anyway to try this show out. Then your show finishes, you might have enjoyed it... but then you stick some music on and suddenly your ears are frazzled because the loudness jumps back up to the standard and you have set your headphones too high. This is what we are trying to avoid by sticking to a standardised loudness.

This isn't measured in dB. DeciBels refer to a specific point in time, so a podcast might peak at −2dB, with lows of −60dB. Loudness is measured across the entire show, allowing for differences in level across a show. You can have quiet and loud segments while still achieving a good overall loudness, allowing for much more creative freedom.

So, how do we measure loudness?

The global standard is Loudness Unit Full Scale (LUFS), or if you are in the USA and Canada Loudness, K-weighted, relative to full scale (LKFS). These are exactly the same thing.[4]

The only difference is that LUFS is easier to say as a word.

LUFS/LKFS are measured in the negative, so −15 LUFS is louder than −20 LUFS. The "full scale" part of the acronym, like deciBels Full Scale (dBfs), means that 0 is the absolute maximum loudness achievable.

We talk about differences in loudness as Loudness Units (LU). So, −15 LUFS is 5 LU louder than −20 LUFS.

One LU is equivalent to 1dB though, it's just measured over different time periods.

Loudness Range (LRA) is the difference between the quietest and loudest parts of a measured period. This is a clever measurement, in that it excludes the top 5% and the lowest 10% of the total LRA, which stops the LRA reading being affected by silences between segments or one extreme peak. This is measured in LU.

Standards

The industry standard for podcasts is −16 LUFS overall loudness. That's what Apple Podcasts asks for.[1] They also state a tolerance of +/−1, so your show can happily sit at −15 LUFS or −17 LUFS and be considered within the industry norm.

Spotify and a few other streaming services ask for −14 LUFS[2] overall loudness; however, this is for audio in general so it includes pop music, which is typically pretty compressed and goes through a lot of additional mastering. −14 LUFS is quite difficult to achieve for most podcasts.

Broadcast radio is set much lower at −23 LUFS.[3]

How do I know what loudness my show is?

Some DAWs come with a loudness metre built in – Adobe Audition has a great one that shows the loudness over both the long term and the short term in this pretty graphic format (Figure 5.3).

You can see the overall loudness reading in the bottom right and the LRA in the bottom left. The coloured radar shows the short-term loudness over a chosen period of time. Make sure you've tweaked the settings so that your target loudness is −16 LUFS as Audition defaults to −24 LUFS for broadcast.

Hindenburg also has a loudness metre built in.

There are free loudness metres online if you work in a DAW that doesn't come with one, but you do get what you pay for, so it is worth getting a decent one if you are getting serious about podcast production.

Figure 5.3 LUFS radar.

You'll only know the overall loudness once you've done the final mix and master, then analysed the final file. Depending on your mastering process, it is likely your mix will be around −18 LUFS, but with some additional tweaking of the final file you can bring it up to −16 LUFS.

One of the reasons I use Audition is that it has great loudness analysis built in. As well as the loudness radar, which analyses in real time, you can analyse the whole file at once. To do this, open up your file in the waveform editor. Switch to the "mastering and analysis" workspace (Window > Workspace > Mastering and Analysis) and a box titled "Amplitude Statistics" appears in the lower right. Select the entire file, click scan and after a bit of processing time a bunch of useful statistics will appear in that window – the most important is the one at the bottom, confusingly titled "ITU BS.1770–3 Loudness: xxxx LUFS". This is your programme loudness!

Monitor loudness while you edit and mix

When we refer to programme loudness we are talking about the entire show, but your metre still reads short-term loudness too. That's how you aim for −16 LUFS cross the whole show – by knowing what your short-term loudness is in your loud and quiet parts.

Use your host's voice-over as your loudness anchor point and mix that to −16 LUFS (or −19 if it is in mono), then balance all your other audio around that.

Keep checking your loudness metre. It's really easy to drift up or down over the course of a show, but remember that it is totally OK for a quiet part to read −25 LUFS and a loud part to read −10 LUFS, as long as these parts are intended to be that loud or quiet and your anchor point, your voice-over, is still around the −16 mark.

Mono vs stereo

Mono files sound louder than stereo files by about 3 LU, so if your podcast is, for whatever reason, in mono only you should be aiming for −19 LUFS across the whole show.

Levels

To achieve that key loudness level of −16 LUFS, we need to balance all our audio to appropriate levels. This is a mix of art and science. Mixing is very subjective, but there are a few key things you are trying to achieve when you're levelling:

- No clipping
- Consistency
- Overall loudness of −16 LUFS
- A show that sounds great

Let's break that down…

No clipping means that you need to keep your peaks below 0dBfs. In fact, I usually aim to keep them below −2dBfs just for safety. If your audio peaks too high, it will clip, cutting off the peak of the waveform and cause distortion – and I don't mean that chunky distortion you hear from overdriven guitar amps. This is ugly digital distortion that is really unpleasant to hear.

You should be achieving good levels at the recording stage, then compensating for high peaks and low level segments with volume automation to smooth it out.

Consistency is really where the art comes in. Your listener shouldn't have to touch their volume controls at all while they are listening, but you also need to preserve some dynamic range – some difference between loud and quiet.

It is really easy to just stick a high ratio, low threshold compressor across the entire mix and flatten the levels out entirely. If you want to hear what this sounds like, check out old episodes of "Harmontown", Dan Harmon's live recorded podcast. The levels are even but it is really harsh and tiring on your ears.

So you want your volume levels to be consistent... but not flat. Somewhere in between that makes the show sound natural and dynamic without being a chore to listen to.

Overall loudness of −16 LUFS is the goal to be within industry standards[1] and does actually require quite a lot of work at the mixing stage to bring everything up to levels that will achieve −16 without causing clipping. You probably won't get to −16 LUFS on your first mix. That's OK – it's a target to aim for; as long as you are keeping an eye on it while making your show sound great, then you're on the right track.

A show that sounds great is by far the most important of these things and it is easy to lose sight (sound?) of that when you are trying to stick to industry standards and boost everything up to −16 LUFS. If your show sounds amazing but has only reached −18 LUFS, then really don't sacrifice the overall balance of your show trying to get those extra 2 LU. Maybe you just have more quiet passages than most shows. If the overall balance is great and you're sort of in the ballpark for loudness, then nobody is going to come at you and throw a big book of podcast rules across the room. We're all just aiming to make great shows here.

So where do we start with levelling?

Good question. How about we make sure our audio is all peaking at the same level, getting it in the right ballpark.

We do that by **Normalising** our audio files. Normalising is a blunt force tool which finds the highest peak in an audio file and adjusts the level of the entire file so that particular peak is a certain level. It doesn't affect the dynamic range, it doesn't do anything fancy at all. It's just useful for getting all our audio into a place where we can start doing the real work.

Normalise each audio file you are using to −2dB. This will keep any peaks below 0dBfs while leaving just a little headroom in case you do add in any processing later that does lift the levels a bit. If you're working with a stereo file, make sure you set it to normalise all channels equally, otherwise you might end up messing up the stereo image.

In Audition you do this in the waveform editor. Select the whole file, click Effects > Amplitude and Compression > Normalise.

Remember that this process is destructive, so it is important to have backups of your original files saved elsewhere.

Voice-over

Start with the voice-over. This is your anchor point. Aim for it to be peaking between −12dB and −6dB, with the loudness metre reading around −16 LUFS in short-term loudness.

It's pretty unlikely you will achieve −16 LUFS with gain and overall volume alone, which is where automation comes in. Set your overall volume so that your audio is mostly peaking in the target zone of −12dB and −6dB, then just like we covered in the chapter on editing, go through your voice-over track using automation to bring down the higher peaks that would cause clipping. Bring up the quieter parts that are harder to hear.

Voice-over won't usually be too dynamic, so you shouldn't have to get too extreme with the automation. You'll mostly be making cuts and boosts of 3dB–6dB (Figure 5.4).

You're aiming for a relatively even level here. If you want your voice-over to be pretty punchy, then you'll also apply compression later on in the mixing stage.

Levelling interviews

When you're levelling interviews, the volume will be naturally more dynamic as the conversation changes topics and because the host and guest will be interacting in a more organic way than when reading a voice-over script. You might have to apply automation boosts and cuts of up to 15dB.

To keep the interview more natural sounding, apply your changes in volume to whole passages of speech, perhaps just adding smaller, more granular changes around particular peaks. That way, the natural dynamic of individual words or sentences is preserved while keeping the programme loudness within industry standards.

Remember to keep an eye on your loudness metre as well as the level metres. You don't want your signal to be hitting the red at any stage of the chain.

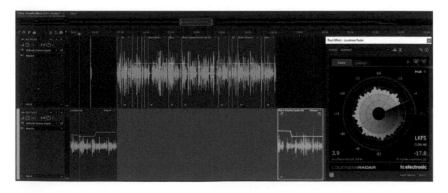

Figure 5.4 Voice-over automation with radar.

With multiple people involved, make sure to check the volume of each person against each other as well. Just skip between the two and listen to see if one is noticeably louder than the other.

You should also, where possible, **cut microphones that aren't in use.** Use automation to fade the audio right out. This is because if you have multiple people speaking in the same room, no matter how well you have positioned your mics they are going to pick up bleed, which will make your recording sound echoey. Each open mic also introduces more noise and headphone bleed too.

If your interview was recorded somewhere with atmospheric noise (i.e. not in a studio), then you will need to be somewhat artful with fading these mic channels in and out. If the drop in ambient noise is jarring, try using the wildtrack you hopefully recorded on location to fill the gap.

Compression and other dynamic controls

Compression is one of the most useful tools in your effects processing rack. It's also one of the most misunderstood and toughest to master.

A compressor is a tool to reduce the dynamic range of an audio signal. It's going to be something you use a whole lot.

That's the short and simple definition. It squashes your audio so that it goes from something that looks like this (Figure 5.5):

To this … (Figure 5.6):

I'm sure you're wondering why you just spent all that time reading a chapter on how to sort your levels out when you can just stick a compressor on the channel which will do it for you… well, compression does do some of the work, but if you overapply it, then you lose the natural dynamism of speech.

That can be a good thing when used as an effect. A voice-over can be made to sound fat and punch with some creatively applied compression,

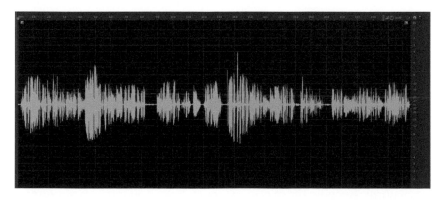

Figure 5.5 Uncompressed wave.

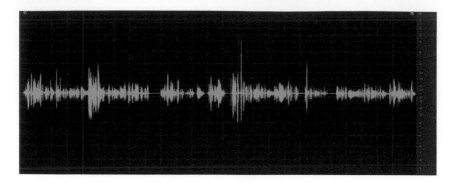

Figure 5.6 Compressed wave.

but voice-over is supposed to sound a little artificial. It is a kind of acting. If you go over the top with compression on an interview, then it will sound unnatural.

Long periods of overly compressed audio are also tiring for a listener's ears and can sound harsh.

Compressors work by reducing the level of all audio over a fixed volume threshold. They can also bring the overall level up to compensate.

That sounds pretty simple, but there are more variables at play here than might be first apparent. Let's take a look at the controls on a standard peak compressor.

Threshold: this is the level at which the compressor kicks in.

Ratio: this is how much the compressor reduces the level of the audio over the threshold. The higher the ratio, the more the sound gets squished. When a signal goes over the threshold the difference in decibels is reduced.

Let's say the threshold is set to −20dB, with the ratio set quite high at 5:1. We have an uncompressed signal that peaks at −15dB. When we turn the compressor on, this peak has passed the threshold by 5dB. The ratio of 5:1 means that 5dB becomes 1dB, so the signal now peaks at −19dB.

Attack: how quickly the compressor kicks in once the signal passes the threshold. It's pretty common for this to be set as low as possible so that the compressor starts working instantly. If you want to preserve the peaks though, this can be turned up a little to around 5ms–10ms (milliseconds).

Release: how quickly the compressor stops reducing level once the signal drops back below the threshold. A short release of around 80ms–120ms will create a beefy, punchier sound; however, this can also sound less natural. Keeping the release longer at 200ms–300ms or will preserve natural dynamics more but is also less punchy.

Make-up gain: if you only brought the peaks down, you would reduce the overall level of the audio, so the make-up gain controls how much the compressor brings up the overall level of the audio. This can often be set to auto, to automatically match the reduction in amplitude the compressor applies.

Peak or RMS

This setting doesn't appear on all compressors. Where it does appear, it refers to how the compressor reads when the signal crosses the threshold. "Peak" is the standard, referring to when the peaks cross the threshold. In this mode the compressor will respond every time the signal passes the threshold.

"Root Mean Squared" (RMS) refers to the average level of the signal, so the compressor will allow some peaks to pass the signal threshold without responding as long as the average level of the signal is below a certain level. This is a more natural sounding compression as it is applied over a longer period, but will also allow for some peaks that you might not want.

If you're still struggling, imagine that you're playing loud music... or perhaps, blasting out the latest episode of *The Daily*. Michael Barbaro's soothing tones are echoing through the walls of your house. Your dad, however, is more of a *Wall Street Journal* kind of guy, and once *The Daily* gets too loud he's going to come and shout at you to turn it down. The point at which it gets too loud for your dad is the threshold of the compressor. How quickly your dad gets to your room to shout at you is the attack. How much you turn it down is the ratio and how long it takes for you to turn it back up again after your dad has left is the release.

Side chain

Lots of compressors also have a second input called a side chain. This allows the compressor's gain reduction to be triggered by a separate signal. This tends to be used more in music production than in podcasts. For example, if you wanted the bass drum to cut through over guitars, you could rig a compressor to be triggered by the drum, bringing the guitars down with every beat (Figure 5.7).

You should make sure you've really mastered the other controls on the compressor before experimenting with the side chain.

One use for the side chain in podcasts is if you are working on an interview that needs to be published really quickly or you just want to get a rough draft to someone, then you could put a compressor on each microphone with a really low threshold and high ratio, then have it triggered by a side chain from the other microphone. This is a quick and dirty way to cut out some bleed.

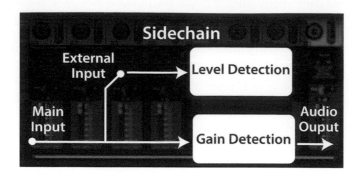

Figure 5.7 Sidechain diagram.

Limiters

You might come across a limiter or there might be a limiter setting in your compressor. This is a version of a compressor designed to stop audio ever going above a certain level, for example, to stop speakers blowing out in a concert venue, or in a podcast producer's case as a final safety measure on your master bus to keep everything below 0dBfs.

A limiter isn't really a different thing, it is just a peak compressor with the ratio turned way up though, to at least 20:1, going all the way up to infinity:1.

How to use a compressor

Voice-over should cut through your mix cleanly, especially if you are running it over music. Just how heavily you compress your voice-over will depend on personal preference and the style of your podcast, but most producers tend to go for a more compressed sound on their voice-over, but not overcompressed. Aim for a rounded, punchy sound – but remember this is a podcast, we're talking more NPR and less commercial top 40 radio. A quicker release will fatten the sound up and a short attack applies the compressor to the whole wave.

Voice-over starting settings cheat sheet:

- Threshold: −8dB
- Ratio: 3.5:1
- Attack: 0.2ms
- Release: 130ms
- Peak mode

Interview audio should be more natural sounding than your voice-over. Most of your dynamic control should be mainly done through levelling.

You could either try a lower threshold with a more gentle ratio such as 2:1 here to reduce the overall dynamic, or you could set the threshold just to catch the higher amplitudes and reduce those with a moderate ratio of 3:1. RMS mode is often more useful for the interview, especially if you are manually lowering the peaks with automation already. Keep the attack and release longer to preserve natural transient dynamics.

Interview Compressor cheat sheet:

- Threshold: −6dB
- Ratio: 2:1
- Attack: 0.6ms
- Release: 200ms
- RMS mode.

Music has already been mixed and mastered so you shouldn't compress it at all. Control your dynamics manually.

Actuality

You should be preserving the dynamics of actuality even more than your interview audio, but you might still want to squash it a little. Compression brings the noise floor up, so any atmospheric noise or things happening in the background of the desired part of the audio is going to be emphasised.

Actuality Compressor cheat sheet:

- Threshold: −8dB
- Ratio: 2:1
- Attack: 0.6ms
- Release: 220ms
- RMS mode

The master bus

Depending on how you master your final mix you might want to put a compressor on your master output. If you do that, be careful. Double compressing audio can make it harsh and tiring for the listener, especially over long periods... such as the duration of a podcast. If you do choose to put a compressor on your master bus, then you should use it more as a limiter to catch any rogue peaks that your other channel compressors haven't caught. Set your threshold high, around −2dB. Use a very quick attack as close to instant as possible and a moderate release. With a ratio around 5:1, you should stop most things from clipping. If you still have clipping, then there are other problems with your levels that you should go back and fix!

Actuality Compressor cheat sheet:

- Threshold: −2dB
- Ratio: 5:1
- Attack: 0.0ms (Instant)
- Release: 150ms
- Peak mode

These cheat sheets are all suggestions. Compression is a subtle art that needs a lot of practice to master. It can ruin a mix just as easily as it can make it great.

Compression is one form of dynamic control. Lumped alongside compressors you might see some others that are less useful for podcasting, but still helpful to know about.

An **expander** does the opposite of a compressor and increases the dynamic range of a signal. You get both upward and downward expanders. With downward expanders, just like the compressor, it reduces the signal's amplitude by a fixed ratio; however, instead of applying this reduction any time the signal goes over the threshold, it applies the reduction whenever it is *under* the threshold. A downward expander can be a useful way to reduce background noise when noise reduction software isn't doing the trick.

Upward expanders increase the amplitude above the threshold. If you can find a use for this, email me because it seems pointless.

Gating is the expander version of limiting. Anything below a certain threshold gets cut entirely. These are really useful for live sound engineers, but in your podcast mix it is better to cut channels yourself when they're not in use. That way, you don't get any rogue coughs or table thuds sneaking into your final mix.

EQ and clarity

EQ is another tool you will use a lot of. You'll probably have some form of EQ on almost every single piece of audio you use.

Sounds such as speech are made up of lots of waves at different frequencies. EQ is the process of altering the balance of frequencies within an audio signal. If you've ever used a piece of audio equipment like a guitar amp or stereo hi-fi that lets you control the bass, mid and treble, then that is a very basic form of EQ.

The name equalization is a hangover from its application in electronics and telecommunications. We aren't aiming for a flat frequency spectrum signal in podcast production.

The use of an EQ is either corrective or creative. You can change the way something sounds purely for aesthetic, creative reasons, tweaking just the right parts of a voice that makes a listener find a voice sound more pleasant. You can also use EQ to correct problems with audio, to remove unwanted hiss, plosive pops or ground rumble, for example.

When you are applying EQ, follow these steps:

- Listen to your audio
- Decide what you want to do to it
- Apply the filters
- Listen again, turning the EQ on and off to compare it with and without

What is an equaliser?

An EQ is a set of filters that allow you to cut or boost certain ranges of frequencies. Each filter will have the following controls:

- **Freq** is the centre frequency of the band you are boosting or cutting.
- **Gain** is the amount by which you are boosting or cutting that range.
- **Q**, quality factor, is the width of the band of frequencies you are modifying. The higher this number is, the narrower the band.
- **Type** is what type or shape of filter you will use. This may not appear on the EQ you are using, in which case the type of each filter is fixed.

Types of filter

Band Filters:

Filters which only boost a certain band around a chosen frequency are the core component of an EQ. You'll probably use 2–4 of these on each EQ.

Proportional Q vs Constant Q:

Band filters with proportional Q change the Q value depending on how much gain you apply. Constant Q keeps the Q value the same, so bandwidth variations are smaller. Proportional Q tends to be a little more natural sounding so is better for creative EQ applications, whereas constant Q is better for corrective use, especially when removing specific frequency noises.

Bell or notch:

Usually called a "bell" or a "notch" to refer to different shapes. You can also have "**band shelf**", which creates a broad, flat boost in a "shelf" shape.

High shelf and low shelf

A high shelf cuts or boosts the gain of everything above a certain frequency, creating a "shelf" pattern on the EQ graph (Figure 5.8).

A low shelf does the same, but for everything below a certain frequency.

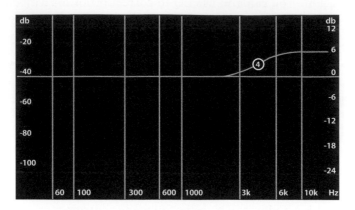

Figure 5.8 EQ high shelf.

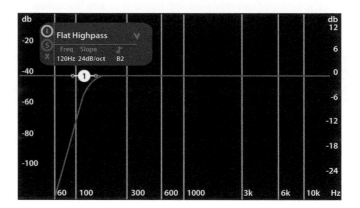

Figure 5.9 EQ high-pass.

With shelf filters, the frequency control is the midpoint of the slope, and when you adjust the Q on this type of filter you are changing how steep the slope is.

High-pass or low-pass

As the name suggests, a high-pass filter only allows the signal content above a certain frequency through. Some producers call this a low cut or a roll off to avoid confusion, as high-pass filters are often placed at the lower end of the spectrum so the name can feel a little counterintuitive. The opposite is true of a low-pass (Figure 5.9).

These often have a "slope" control instead of a Q control, measured in dB/octave. The higher the dB/octave, the steeper the slope.

A high-pass is really useful as a corrective measure to take out things like low-end wind noise, ground rumble and the most intrusive parts of plosive pops. It is a slope rather than a cliff, so if you need to take out something that is around, for example, 60Hz, you would need to set the freq control higher (around 100Hz with a 48dB/Oct slope).

A low-pass is similarly useful correctively to take out hiss; however, this can dull your sound down so it's best used when there is nothing desirable above that certain frequency, such as if you are using audio from a phone call.

Parametric or graphic

So far we have been talking about parametric EQ because this is the kind of EQ that is most useful to podcast producers. Parametric EQs tend to have between three and ten filters with a freq, Q and possibly type control for each.

A graphic EQ has fixed frequency filters; however, there are usually far more with most units having between ten and 30 filters. These are popular in live sound installations and are often used to shape the sound of an entire mix to compensate for how a particular space might sound without it.

That isn't a rule though, if you have a graphic EQ you really like using, then nothing is stopping you.

Creative EQ

The process of using EQ purely to make something sound nicer is called creative EQ. There is plenty of crossover between creative and corrective EQ – correcting something will make it sound better, after all.

When you're first starting to EQ something, you won't be familiar with what altering different parts of the frequency spectrum does to that sound. There is a trick you can do to get familiar quickly though, called a **filter sweep**.

To do this, take an otherwise flat EQ, select one of the band filters, turn the Q up pretty high – around 5.0 – turn the gain up to at least 10dB and then while you play out the audio, sweep it across the frequency spectrum. Some EQs let you drag the filter within the graphic display itself, otherwise just start with the frequency at 20Hz and turn it up until you get past 16,000Hz.

Listen carefully to how the sound changes as you slowly sweep the frequency up. It doesn't have to be one smooth movement, you are just getting used to the different parts of the sound.

By doing this, you will hear what an extreme boost does to each part of the spectrum and your ears will be more prepared to hear those subtle changes you are going to make.

As you get more adept at using EQ, you'll be able to pinpoint which frequencies you want to work with without using the filter sweep, but even seasoned audio engineers use this technique to seek out problematic frequencies.

EQing speech

When applying EQ to speech, you are aiming for it to be clear and intelligible with some subtle enhancements to make it more pleasing to the human ear.

This is a rough guide to which parts of the frequency spectrum do what in the human voice:

0Hz–60Hz: rumble. Often content that isn't useful.

60Hz–120Hz: this is where the bass warmth of someone with a deep voice can be felt.

150Hz–400Hz: if your voice is sounding a little muddy, try a cut in this range, centred on 250Hz.

1,900Hz–2,300Hz: boosts in this range can be used to enhance the "bite" of a voice.

1,500Hz–5000Hz: this is where most of the intelligibility and clarity of speech is; 3,000–5,000 can also add some brightness.

4,000Hz–6,000Hz: boosting in this area can add some presence or if your voice is sounding a little harsh, sibilant or thin, then try a subtle cut in this range.

6,000Hz and upwards: boosting in this range can add an "airy" quality, creating a brighter overall sound to the voice.

You can start from a flat, default EQ and use this guide to make adjustments to your speech audio.

This is just a guide though, everyone's voice is different. Subtlety is important, so you are only usually making adjustments of 1dB–4dB. Once you go above that, it starts sounding too obvious and unnatural and the listener will wonder why the voice has an "effect" on it.

As with compression, you should be more subtle with your interview recordings than you are with your voice-over. Depending on the format you are likely to be listening to the interview for much longer than the voice-over as well, so anything too unnatural could become harsh and tiring to listen to over time.

Once you have applied your EQ, play the audio back with the EQ turned on, and turn it off then on again so you can hear the difference. It might be more obvious than you think with small adjustments once you compare it this way.

Cheat sheets

Here are some settings you can use as a starting point for your speech EQ.

Voice-over

This should give you a crisp, bright voice. All voices are different, so you should tweak it once you have applied these.

Each number refers to a different filter, applied in a parametric EQ:
1. High-Pass Filter (flat)

- Freq: 100Hz
- Slope: 24dB/Oct

This cuts out generally unwanted low-end content that is often barely audible anyway, allowing for extra headroom in the overall signal.
2. Proportional Q band filter

- Freq: 250Hz
- Gain: −3dB
- Q: 2.0

This filter removes some muddiness from the voice.
3. Proportional Q band filter

- Freq: 2,250Hz
- Gain: + 4dB
- Q: 1.5

Adds a little bit of "bite" in the mid-range.
4. Proportional Q band filter

- Freq: 5,250Hz
- Gain: −1dB
- Q: 1.2

Subtly removes some high mid-harshness.
5. High Shelf filter

- Freq: 7,750Hz
- Gain: + 3dB
- Q: 1.0

Boosts the top end, adding brightness and air.

Interview guest

These are very similar settings to the voice-over cheat sheet, except softened up a little to make it easier.
1. High-Pass Filter (flat)

- Freq: 100Hz
- Slope: 48dB/Oct

Just like in the voice-over, this cuts out unwanted low-end noise, but with a steeper slope. Interviews are more likely to have noise introduced by subjects moving around or with poor mic technique, so this should help with noise and plosive pops.

2. Proportional Q band filter

- Freq: 250Hz
- Gain: –2dB
- Q: 2.0

This filter removes some muddiness from the voice, but with a smaller dip than on the voice-over.

3. Proportional Q band filter

- Freq: 2,000Hz
- Gain: + 2dB
- Q: 1.2

For the interview, we can still add just a little mid-range bite but the Q is lowered here, broadening the affected range and the frequency slightly lower as well, just to keep things a little softer and more natural.

4. High Shelf filter

- Freq: 6,000Hz
- Gain: + 1.5dB
- Q: 1.0

For the interview guest, we can start the high shelf a little lower but not turn it up as much, keeping this a little more natural and less likely to cause ear fatigue across a lengthy interview.

EQing actuality

Your actuality is likely very varied, so you're really going to have to use your ears here, but really watch out for the low-end, especially with recordings made outside.

If you are rolling actuality underneath your voice-over or interviews, then avoid boosting frequencies associated with clarity in speech. This will keep that part of the mix free for your speech, allowing it to remain intelligible.

Common noise issues that can be solved with EQ are:

- Wind, below 150Hz
- Mains hum: 50Hz or 60Hz depending on which country you are in
- Plosive pops: below 150Hz

As you can see, a lot of unwanted noise is in the lower frequencies, so it's pretty common to just stick a high-pass filter at about 100Hz.

Corrective EQ

EQ can be used to find and remove or at least de-emphasise unwanted parts of the frequency content. This is known as corrective EQ. Probably the most common (and easy to apply) use of corrective EQ is using a high-pass filter at around 100Hz to remove a raft of problems:

- Plosive pops
- Wind noise
- Ground rumble and handling noise

If you can hear a noise in your audio that is likely to only be within a narrow frequency band, such as a hum or constant whine, then you can probably remove it with corrective EQ. Use the **filter sweep** technique, described above, to find the problematic noise and then cut that range entirely with a narrow (high) Q value.

Lots of noise spans different parts of the frequency spectrum, so if you have dedicated noise reduction software, then that might be more useful for fixing up audio than just relying on corrective EQ. That's covered in the chapter on noise reduction and fixing up messy audio.

EQ as an effect

Sometimes you might want to play with your audio to create a certain effect. A common one would be to make something sound really tinny to imitate it coming from a small TV or radio set. To do this, you just add a high-pass filter and roll it up to about 600Hz, then a low-pass filter at about 4,000Hz, with a boost of 6dB–8dB between 2,000Hz and 3,500Hz.

Common mistakes

Overdoing it: EQ should be used subtly. Most of the adjustments you make will be between 0.5dB and 6dB. The effect will be overall pretty subtle if you do it right.

Using the same settings on every voice: try to boost different frequency ranges in each speaker. There is a balance to be struck between consistency of sound and giving each voice its own space in the frequency spectrum.

Too much top end: large boosts to the high-mid/high part of the frequency spectrum (6,000Hz and upwards) are immediately pleasing to the ear. You instantly get more air and a brighter sound. It's really tempting to just boost the top end by a large amount as it can sound really sparkly and bright, but too much of this region can become harsh to listen to over time.

Using your eyes: the graphical display on software-based parametric EQs is really helpful in knowing exactly what you are doing, but it is easy to rely on it and forget to actually listen to what you are doing.

Ignoring context: compare what you are EQing to other channels you have EQed. Does everyone involved in an interview sound consistent? If one has loads of bass and another has loads of top end, then it is going to be jarring.

Noise reduction and how to clean up bad audio

Getting the recording right at the source will always be the best way to make a great podcast, but especially in the haphazard world of podcasting we are often working with imperfect situations and imperfect audio. There is an arsenal of tricks we can use as producers to fix up audio and get it as close to studio quality as is possible.

Remote recording is also becoming more and more common, so we producers find ourselves in less control of the space in which our interviewees are recording. It's far from ideal, but we need to be able to compensate for this.

This is where your audio manipulation skills are going to go a bit CSI-esque.

The automatic way: noise reduction software

Noise reduction is the process of using software to detect and remove unwanted noise from your audio. This noise could be mains hum, air conditioning or even a phone message tone.

Some digital audio workstations come with noise reduction built in, but as a podcast producer a good noise reduction plug-in is one of the best investments you'll make. With the right software, noise reduction is remarkably easy, but to people unfamiliar with audio production it is also particularly impressive.

The way most noise reduction software works boils down to the software being fed a short sample of the noise that's trying to be removed and then comparing that to the audio signal and subtracting it, in theory leaving only the speech.

That's the most simple versions; there is also algorithmic software that "learns" as the audio plays, allowing it to adapt to shifting ambient noise.

What can be removed this way

- The more consistent the sound, the better automatic noise reduction will be at removing it.
- The narrower the frequency band the noise covers, the easier it is to remove.

What can't be removed

- Inconsistent sound, such as someone else talking over your interviewee or a dog barking in the background.
- Sound that shares the same parts of the frequency spectrum as the audio you want to keep.
- Broadband noise (covering large parts of the frequency spectrum) will result in degraded audio quality no matter what you do.

What's the catch?

Noise reduction isn't perfect at all. It will remove at least a small part of the audio you want to keep. The more noise that is being removed the harder the software finds it to distinguish between "good" audio and "bad", so in really badly noisy audio the software can introduce a lot of audio artefacts that make the voice sound strange and digital. It can also remove so much of the desired sound that what's left sounds thin and weak. Most noise reduction software allows you to listen to the noise you are removing so you can hear for yourself just how much of the desired audio you are taking out.

Controls found in noise reduction software

- **Learn/Capture Noise Print**: select a region of your audio that is just noise and click this to load an example of the undesired noise into your noise reduction software.
- **Reduction Amount**: as you might expect, this is how much you want to reduce noise by. If your noise reduction software is working perfectly, then turn this all the way up. If it's removing some of the audio you want to keep, then you need to find a balance by toying with this setting.
- **Threshold**: the amplitude below which noise reduction happens. If you turn this right up, noise reduction will always be in play or you can set it at an appropriate level for your speech (start with −15dB), and then noise reduction will only occur in the gaps between speech.
- **Spectral Decay Rate**: this is the percentage of frequencies processed when audio falls below the noise floor. Tweaking this is a balance between allowing some noise to remain (when set at higher percentage values) and introducing more burbling audio artefacts (when this is set at lower values).
- **Smoothing**: another control for balancing artefacts against background noise. Higher values reduce artefacts at the expense of higher levels of noise.

How to use noise reduction

- **Capture the noise you want to remove**. Most noise reduction software will have a button that says something like "learn" or "capture noise print". Select a part of your audio that contains just noise (this is another reason capturing wildtrack is important!) and click this button.

- **Apply the noise reduction to your track**.
- **Gradually raise the threshold control from zero until you don't hear any noise**. This way, you don't remove more audio content than necessary.
- **Preview the noise reduction**. If you are doing your processing in a destructive editor, such as Audition's waveform view, then you will want to preview the sound first. Let it play.
- **Tweak the settings**. Play around with the settings until you get a good balance between noise removal and introducing artefacts.
- **Listen to "noise only"**. Most noise reduction software has a setting to check what you are actually removing. Check this out to make sure you aren't removing too much of the sound you want to keep
- **Apply**

If you're editing in Adobe Audition or Izotope RX 7, then you can use the spectral editor when you're capturing your noise print, allowing you to only select noise within a specific frequency band. Your noise reduction will then leave the rest of the frequency spectrum untouched.

The manual way

Sometimes automatic noise reduction doesn't quite cut it, and in some scenarios it's just easier to sharpen your audio scalpel and perform some sound surgery.

Manual noise removal is better suited to short duration noises such as phone message tones or plosive pops.

Spectral view

Some audio editors, such as Adobe Audition, Izotope RX 7 and Audacity, allow you to edit in a spectral view. Plug-ins are available for other DAWs like Pro-Tools to enable this as well. This is your most useful tool for cutting unwanted noise out of some audio.

To access this in Audition, head to the waveform editor (remembering this means you are editing destructively) and click view > Show spectral frequency display (Figure 5.10).

Spectral pitch display will show the frequency content in musical format which can also be useful, but in speech editing the frequency displayed in Hz is more relevant.

The spectral editor shows more information than the waveform editor. Where the waveform editor only shows the overall amplitude of the whole wave, the spectral editor breaks it down and shows the amplitude of each frequency.

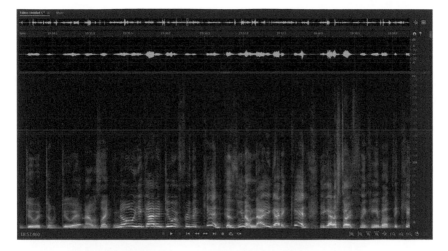

Figure 5.10 Spectral view.

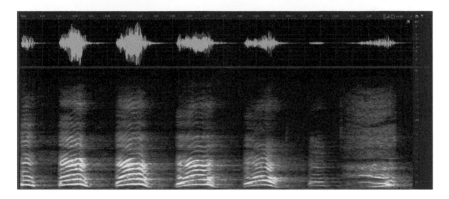

Figure 5.11 Spectral laugh.

It looks a bit like a heat map or like you are looking at something through thermal goggles. That's actually a really useful way to think of it because it's not far off the truth.

Just like in the waveform editor the X-axis is time; however, the Y-axis isn't amplitude, it is frequency. The spectral view displays higher amplitudes as brighter patches. Silence is black (Figure 5.11).

This is a recording of a guest laughing, recorded into an iPhone. Because it is an iPhone recording straight to M4A format, there is nothing above 16KHz. You can also see that on the first laugh, represented by the first of the three bursts, there is a blast of low frequency content – likely to be a plosive pop.

Using the Marquee editor (the one that looks like a dotted square) you can drag and select parts of the frequency spectrum across a specific time. Hit play and you'll hear what you have selected... if it is all audio you want to get rid of, hit delete.

You can see in this example that there was a low bandwidth noise at around 2kHz for a short period of time (somebody got a text message) (Figure 5.12).

By selecting it with the marquee editor and hitting delete, we can remove this part of the frequency spectrum (Figure 5.13).

If you hover your mouse cursor over the Y-axis which displays frequency to the right of the spectral editor, you can use the mousewheel

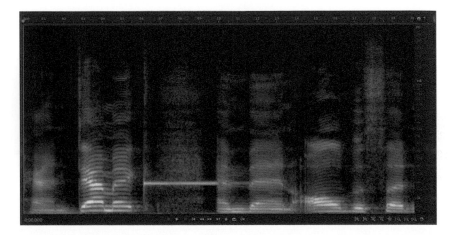

Figure 5.12 Spectral phone noise.

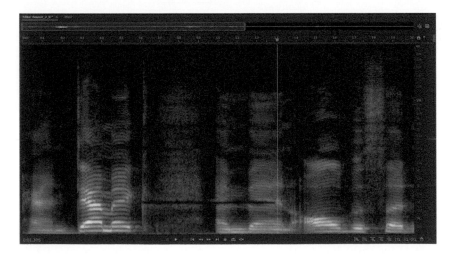

Figure 5.13 Spectral phone noise gone.

to zoom in and out, then click and drag to focus on different parts of the spectrum.

There is, of course, no way to distinguish between "good" frequency content and "bad". If a phone dings creates a burst of sound in the 2KHz–2.5KHz range, you can delete it... but you are deleting everything in that range for that time period, so you'll lose those frequencies from what you intended to record as well. You can see that in the example above there is a dark gap left where the phone noise was removed.

Removing plosive pops

No matter how hard you try and how diligent you are about using pop shields, at some point someone will get too close to the microphone and get a bunch of pops all over your recording.

Luckily this is one of the most routine, easy operations you can perform on your audio patient. It's also one of the most common, and once you've learned how to remove plosive pops you can apply the same techniques to other unwanted noise.

There are three different ways to remove plosive pops:

*   In the multitrack (non-destructive, but less precise)
*   With the spectral editor (destructive)
*   Using EQ (quick, but inaccurate and removes all low-end)

Removing plosives in the multitrack editor

Using this method removes the pop, but as you are removing an entire time selection of audio rather than just a frequency selection it can cause an audible edit.

To remove plosives in the multitrack editor, zoom right in to the plosive. You will see a part of the waveform that looks "stretched", caused by the heavy burst of low frequency content (Figure 5.14).

Switch to your razor tool and cut this out, then stitch the remaining back together with a very short crossfade.

Listen back and make a judgement call on whether you can tell the cut has been made. If you can't, then your work (at least on this pop) is done. If you can tell, then hit the undo button until we're back to where we started. It's time to try another method.

Removing plosives in the spectral editor

As always, make sure you have a backup of your audio before doing any destructive editing.

Open up your audio in the spectral editor and zoom in horizontally to the plosive, but also zoom in vertically to the lower part of the frequency spectrum (Figure 5.15).

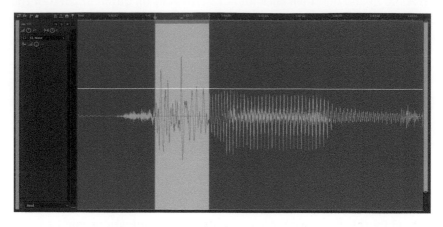

Figure 5.14 Plosive pop.

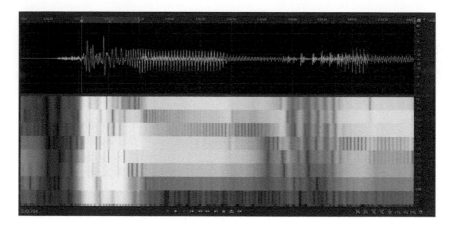

Figure 5.15 Plosive pop in spectral.

You should see a bright region below 100Hz where the plosive is. Select this with the marquee tool, play it – you should hear a low rumbly burst and not much else. Hit delete, then deselect the region and play the audio back. Your plosive pop should be gone.

If your audio sounds tinny and thin, then you have deleted too much too far up the frequency spectrum. Undo the delete and make sure you are only selecting the region below 100Hz.

If you have the iZotope audio editor, it has a really useful brush tool that you can use to get more surgical with your plosive deletions (Figure 5.16).

The downside to this method is that it can still leave in any higher frequency distortion that is caused by clipping associated with the pop.

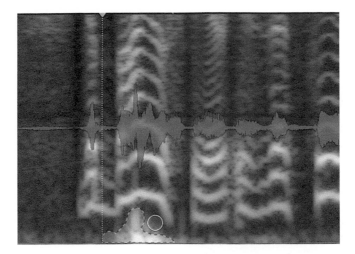

Figure 5.16 Plosive in Izotope.

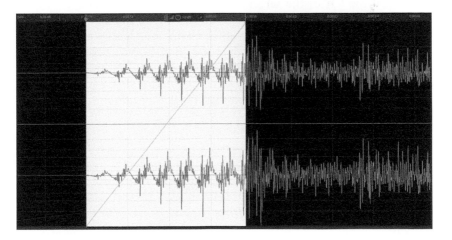

Figure 5.17 Corrective HPF.

Removing plosives with EQ

If the surgical approach is too time-consuming, then there is a quick and dirty option that will do a pretty good job of, if not removing pops entirely, then at least making them less noticeable.

The noise caused by pops is almost entirely in the sub-100Hz range, so you can apply a high-pass filter at 100Hz in your EQ with a steep 48/dB slope and that will take care of most of the work for you (Figure 5.17).

By doing this you are losing all low-end content. This may not be desirable, especially if your speaker has a very low voice and you want to maintain that richness. You are also leaving in any higher frequency distortion that could be caused if a pop overloads your audio equipment causing clipping.

Fixing clipping

Clipping isn't something that is easily restored if it is really bad; however, there is an option buried within Adobe Audition that attempts to reconstruct a clipped waveform. It won't sound as good as if you had just recorded it right in the first place, but sometimes that ship has sailed and you have to work with what you've got.

Load the audio into the waveform editor.

The declipping tool is kind of hidden in Audition. You have to switch to the "Restoration" workspace. You can either do this by clicking "restoration" at the top of the screen, or alternatively hit window > workspace > restoration in the toolbar at the top of the screen.

Now on the left of the screen, where the media browser typically is, there should be a tab that says "diagnostics". Click on this to bring up some extra repair tools. The drop-down menu has "de-clip as an option".

Select the audio you want to repair and click "scan". You should get a list of clipped waves. You can either hit Repair All to quickly get rid of all the problems, or you can click each one individually to jump to it and listen, before clicking again to repair it.

DeEssing

Sometimes your recorded speech can sound wonderful and bright, and you are totally happy with it apart from one thing: sibilant sounds. Those "s" sounds are a bit too prominent with the brightness your EQ has added, they can be harsh to listen to and overpower the rest of the sentence.

You could alter your EQ to take out some top end, but then you lose that overall brightness in the rest of the speech that you worked so hard to achieve.

Or you could use a deEsser. A deEsser is a special type of compressor that only applies to a narrow frequency band (Figure 5.18)

Audition's deEsser has a display which shows the frequency content. This allows you to move your playhead over the sharply sibilant parts of the speech and see a visual representation on where those peaks are. In the example above, you can see the peak between 6KHz and 10KHz, so the frequency band that the deEsser kicks in is around that peak, reducing the amplitude of that frequency band when it goes over the threshold.

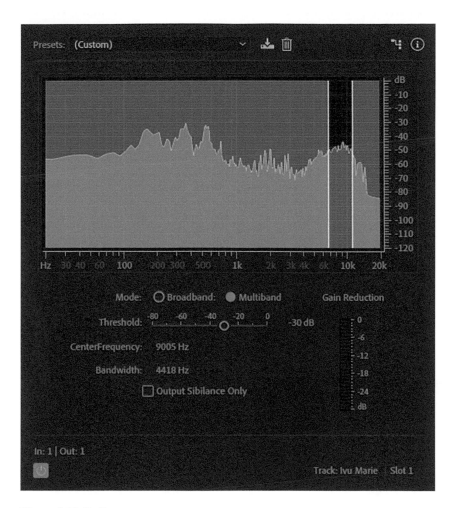

Figure 5.18 DeEsser.

Just like noise reduction, you can listen to the sibilant output only, which is useful for finding and figuring out what needs to be reduced.

More advanced deEssers have more controls, letting you set the threshold, ratio, attack and release – just like a regular compressor.

Reverb

Wherever you are sitting right now clap your hands together and listen for how the sound tails off. That is the reverb of the space. Every room has a unique set of reverberant characteristics.

Reverb is something we've been trying really hard to minimise until now, especially on voice-overs or interviews with guests in their echo-heavy front rooms. It can be distracting.

It can also be really pleasant. Think of a priest giving a sermon at the front of the church – that cavernous space carrying their words right to the back, each sentence drawn out by the long tail of reflected sound, rich with low-end warmth.

So sometimes we want to capture those pleasant reverberations. If your podcast includes part of that sermon, then you can do that really easily by setting up a second microphone further away from the speaker.

Sometimes you might want to get that beautiful churchlike sound without the luxury of having a church to record in. That's where your reverb unit comes in (Figure 5.19).

Most DAWs come with some kind of reverb unit built in. Music producers spend thousands on buying specially tailored hardware units and software plug-ins, because the algorithms within are as unique, variable and subjective as the sound of the individual spaces they emulate.

This book isn't going to advise you to drop a significant portion of your budget on a reverb unit for making podcasts. You can get by without ever using one, but being able to add it as an effect in the right circumstances can add a little extra to your podcast.

Where to use reverb?

Apply artificial reverb sparingly. If you're just doing a straight interview podcast, then you probably won't use it. It's more of a fun effect which you can apply to smooth transitions, extend the tail of a music sting or for occasional comic effect. Avoid it on voice-overs and interviews.

An audio drama however will make liberal use of reverb to simulate the spaces your characters are supposed to be in.

A pretty common technique that producers will use is applying some reverb to newsreel along with a high-pass filter to simulate the sound of a TV in a living room or kitchen.

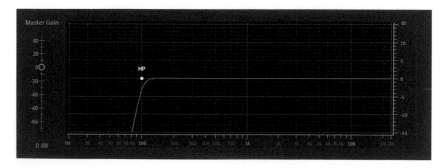

Figure 5.19 Reverb unit.

What do the settings do?

Reverb units are all very different so they won't have all of these settings, but they will have some variation of these parameters to play with.

Type

Type picks the kind of space the reverb is modelled on. Common types are "Hall", "Chamber", "Church" and "Room".

"Plate" and "Spring" are two other common types and emulate common hardware reverb units that were popular in the 1960s for a more vintage sound.

Decay

This is one of the most important settings on the reverb unit. This is how long the reverb "tail" lasts for, usually measured in milliseconds. There is some overlap between what this and "Room Size" does.

Room size

As you'd expect, this changes the size of the room that the reverb unit is emulating. What this actually does varies from unit to unit but generally increasing it increases the stereo field depth (making the sound "wider"), and in the absence of a "decay" control, this also changes the decay length. This setting will also alter the colour and character of the reverberations. Larger room sizes will sound less metallic, with a longer attack period at the start of the reverb.

Early reflections

Reverberations are made up of two sets of reflections: the long tail or "decay" and the early reflections. The amount of early reflections you add changes how close you want your audio to sound to reflective surfaces.

A bathroom or corridor would have high levels of early reflections, whereas a cathedral would have lower levels of early reflections.

Diffusion

This controls the time between each reflection. Higher diffusion pushes the reverberations closer together creating a smoother sound. Lower diffusion separates them out a little more for more audible discrete echoes. Sometimes this is split into early reflection diffusion and decay diffusion.

Pre-delay

Adds a delay to offset the reverb slightly from the "dry" sound, which can be useful to keep some of the clarity of the original sound or to create the impression of a larger space.

Damping

Turning this up takes some of the higher frequencies out of the reverb progressively, creating the impression of a room with surfaces that are less reflective. Turning damping right down gives you a very bright sounding reverb tail; however, this can also be quite harsh in sounds that have a lot of high-end in them to begin with.

High frequency cut

This filters the high frequencies being fed into the reverb unit. If you set it at 4,000Hz, for example, then only sounds below 4,000Hz will be fed into the reverb unit. This is useful if you have any prominent high frequencies that end up overpowering the rest of the sound when it gets to the reverb.

Low frequency cut

This does the same thing as the high frequency cut but at the other end of the spectrum, filtering out lower frequencies that go into the unit. This is particularly useful if your reverb is sounding overly rumbly or muddys up the low-end of your mix.

Wet and dry

As with many other types of effect unit, you have control over how much of the original "dry" signal and the "wet" processed signal make it out the other side of the reverb unit.

If you have your reverb on a send bus, then you should set your wet amount to 100% and your dry amount to 0%. Otherwise this is a creative decision based on what you think sounds best.

Using a send instead of an insert

If you want several pieces of audio on different tracks to sound like they are in the same space, then you can feed them all to the same reverb unit by using a send bus. This is actually a pretty good way of feeding any effect unit where you want to keep some of the original signal in your mix.

To do this, you need to create a new track, but this is a different type of track called a "bus". You create it in the same as other tracks though.

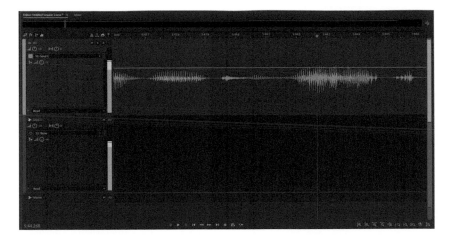

Figure 5.20 Adobe send to bus.

Generally, with reverb, it should be a stereo bus. In Audition it is just clicking Multitrack > Tracks > Add Stereo Bus.

You'll now have a new bus that can be fed audio through sends on other tracks. To do this head to the mixer and on each track, you want to feed audio from, turn the send on and set the level to an appropriate level. In Audition it appears as "S1" on each track (Figure 5.20).

You can then add any effect you like to the effects rack of this track and control the automation and effects parameters just like you would on any other kind of track, but with the ability to feed in audio from multiple sources at once.

Just remember to set your effects to 100% Wet, 0% Dry.

Impulse response reverbs

Some reverb units are known as convolution or impulse response reverbs. These are designed to model specific spaces by loading in a model of a real-life space – that model is an "impulse response". Skilled engineers can go to a space and then create their own impulse response to load into a unit like this, which can then be used to simulate any sound in that space.

Mastering

Mastering is the process of creating your finished audio file: the master copy.

It is the final step of taking all those individual tracks and combining them into one stereo (or occasionally mono) file.

Historically, in the music industry at least mastering has been the lengthy process of comparing each track on an album and making sure they are all around the same loudness and the mixes sound consistent. Then creating a master CD, vinyl record or tape with the tracks in the correct order and the right length of gap (or not) between songs.

Some audio engineers will argue that mastering refers to any processing you apply to the master bus in your final mix. It's a contested term, partly because it is a slightly murky part of the audio industry that a lot of sound engineers don't really dip their toes into.

Mastering a podcast doesn't need to be that complex though.

It's the last step, so check you've done all of the following before you create your master copy:

- Levels and loudness, mixing everything as close to −16LUFS as possible.
- Clean-up: fixed any dodgy audio.
- Creative processing: some compression where it is needed and EQ to make everything sound as good as it possibly can.
- Listened all the way through one last time. If you don't do this, I can guarantee you'll miss something that you should have changed.

Mix it down

There's no need to over-complicate this part – it's just the same as hitting save on a document, but your computer has to do a lot more thinking.

Always export your first master in as high quality as possible, which means you need a WAV file. These are large but completely lossless. It is your master file, so it is good practice to keep it in its original quality, avoiding double compressing – you will convert to MP3 later.

In Pro-Tools you click bounce to disk, in Adobe Audition (and most other DAWs) you hit Export > Multitrack Mixdown, wait a while for your computer to process a huge amount of audio and then... presto, you have a WAV file.

You could convert that to MP3 and publish it, but we're doing a professional job of this, right?

Open up your file in a waveform editor, such as Adobe Audition, and let's make some final adjustments to the file. If you've bought one of the Izotope plug-in packages, then the audio editor that comes with it, RX7, is also good for mastering and analysis.

We're going to be working destructively here, so make a backup of your first WAV file, in case you need to revert. You can also redo the export later, but that is a more time-consuming process than just copying a WAV file.

Ins and outs

To make sure your show plays smoothly on all players, you need to make sure that the audio file starts and ends correctly.

To avoid cutting off the start of the show or stuttering in some players, we need to add half a second of silence at the beginning and end. This is easy enough to do in Adobe Audition, just stick your cursor at the start of the file in the waveform editor and hit edit > insert > silence.

If you're using Audacity, it's generate > silence. In Izotope RX7, you use the signal generator, set to insert mode.

Now that we have silence, we also need to add the tiniest fade at the start, just to make sure your audio doesn't pop as it starts up. Because we are mastering, we are working destructively and applying the fade directly to the audio file, so it is going to look a bit different to all the fades we introduced as part of the editing process.

Your chosen audio editor should have an effect called something like "Fade envelope". In Audition you select the region to apply the fade to and then click effects > amplitude > fade envelope. There's no need to get too fancy on the fade at the start, you're just adding a few milliseconds fade right in the very first chunk of waveform. This is housekeeping, not art. A linear fade will do just fine.

Now do the same at the end – although you might want to make this one a little longer and more artful depending on how your show ends. The important thing is that it reaches silence at a zero crossing point (Figure 5.21).

Peaks

If you've balanced your show perfectly all the way through, it should look relatively even across the entire file. That probably isn't the case though and you can squeeze a little extra loudness out of your show by bringing some of the big peaks down.

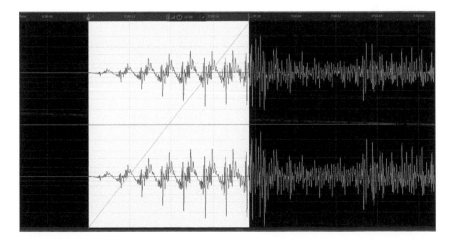

Figure 5.21 Zero crossing master.

You read that right, you need to turn some parts down so that we can make the whole show louder. By removing those peaks, you create "headroom" to allow us to turn up the entire show.

This is definitely a part of the process that is quickest in Audition, because Audition has a really great gain tool in the waveform editor that processes quickly and is really easy to use.

Zoom right out so you can see your whole show in the Waveform editor. You'll probably see a mostly even waveform with the occasional peak that sticks right out. Our goal is to get rid of those peaks, so we're going to repeat this next step for each one.

Select a chunk around the peak – this should be a whole phrase or at least a segment of the audio where a listener is not going to notice a sudden dip in level. In Audition you should have a small gain control hovering around your waveform editor. If you don't, then click View > Show HUD, or hit shift + u to bring it up.

Use this gain control to lower the region's amplitude so it is in line with the rest of the waveform, then listen back to it in context to make sure it sounds even.

The process is similar in Izotope, except that in the "utility" folder to the right of the editor, there is a "gain" process. Click that, turn your gain down and hit render. This is a little slower than Audition's processing and doesn't provide the immediate visual representation that Audition does.

Do this for all the peaks that are as a result of your balance not being perfect – natural changes in dynamic are fine, we just don't want anything that sticks right out.

By the time you're done, you should have a relatively even waveform across the whole file.

You've brought your peaks down, which means we have room to bring the level of the whole file up. To do that, you should normalise the file in the same way you did with all your audio when you first started mixing. Don't normalise to zero – it will sound fine to you but in some players and on some cheaper equipment it may distort on playback; −0.5dB is generally safe.

Applying mastering effects

Many plug-in packages come with some effects processors designed to be run over the final mix as a mastering effect. Be careful with these as they are an easy way to ruin your carefully balanced mix.

They usually have some version of a limiter/compressor and an EQ with spectral analysis built in. There might also be a tool for altering the stereo image, which can be used to add some stereo width to a show that is otherwise mostly mono.

Get good at mastering without plug-ins before you try and use them. That way you'll know what you're aiming for before starting to attempt to take shortcuts. Shortcuts can be important, but if you don't know where you're aiming for you'll end up with an inferior sounding show.

If you do use these plug-ins, use them correctively: just applying a couple of decibels extra gain/cut in the EQ to compensate for peaks and troughs on the whole frequency spectrum.

Once you're confident at mastering, then a quick pass over with a mastering plug-in can be an easy way to create a universal show "sound" across multiple episodes.

Analysis

Let's check the overall loudness! Switch to the mastering and analysis view in Audition, select the whole file and hit "Scan Selection" in the Amplitude Statistics window to the right of the screen. You'll see your overall loudness at the bottom.

If your show is louder than −16LUFS, then don't worry, you can easily lower the amplitude of the entire waveform. Remember 1dB = 1LU, so if your file is coming out at −14.5LUFS, then select the whole file and apply −1.5dB of gain.

Do not try and raise the amplitude of your show in this way to meet −16 LUFS. You'll introduce clipping to your master file.

ID3 tags

One final step you can take with an MP3 file is to add metadata using ID3 tagging software. This metadata can contain an image, which will show up as the file's icon when it is downloaded as well as a description, genre, title, artist and album title.

…you may have gathered that these tags were designed for music, not podcasts.

You can add this metadata super easily using the one of the many ID3 tag editors available online – some are free, all are cheap.

Exercise: remote recording, part 3

Having completed exercises 1 and 2, you should now have two sets of multitrack recordings: your tape-sync style interview audio from exercise 1 and your remote smartphone recording interview from exercise 2.

In this exercise you are going to take all the knowledge you've accumulated, especially in this chapter, and clean up your audio.

Let's start with the remote phone recording. Open up that multitrack session and save a duplicate copy for later.

Part 1: clean-up

Mute the host/interviewer track. For now, let's just focus on the guest.

Go through the audio and identify issues with the recording, then apply the corresponding techniques to resolve them.

Our guest isn't an audio professional – they very rarely are – so you should be making use of at least these three techniques:

- Noise reduction
- Removing plosive pops
- Remove clipping

Remember to A/B your audio when you apply these processes. Check you aren't making your audio worse or introducing too many artefacts.

Listen back to the cleaned up audio and compare it to the original backup copy you saved.

Once you are satisfied you've done the best clean-up job you can, let's do the same for your host/interviewer's track. Mute the guest and unmute the host.

In theory your host, being somewhat more experienced, should have much cleaner audio to start with. You shouldn't need to apply such drastic noise reduction, if any, and the recording might be free of clipping and plosives altogether.

Now listen back to the host's audio in isolation and then again with the interviewee unmuted. Compare to your original recordings and marvel at your newfound technical wizardry.

Part 2: mixing

Now that you have a cleaned up and edited interview, it's time to mix it. The first-half of Chapter 5 will be really useful here.

- Level your audio using gain and automation, aiming for −16LUFS
- EQ
- Compression

This is probably going to be the most dramatic change when you check the original against the mixed version. It should sound noticeably louder and clearer in the new version.

At this stage we've done everything we would do to mix an interview for a podcast!

Part 3: make a master

Let's pretend that the interview we've been working on is our entire podcast and we are ready to master it.

Unmute everything and click export > entire session (if you are in Adobe Audition) to create your WAV file. Use the section on loudness in Chapter 5 to check your overall loudness.

Make a duplicate copy of this file so you can go back if you screw up this part as we are now working destructively.

Still following the guide in Chapter 5 do the following:

• Add 0.5 seconds of silence at the beginning and end
• Add miniscule fades on the start and end of the audio
• Reduce any standout peaks
• Normalise to −0.5dB
• Check the overall loudness again.

If you compare this with your duplicate copy, you probably won't notice much difference. That's fine, the master is a kind of technical housekeeping.

Now save the file as an MP3. You've made a podcast!

Repeat the exercise with the tape-sync style recording for more practice, but pay particular attention to any problems you introduced yourself during exercise 1. You'll be a better tape-syncer for having edited and mixed your own raw tape.

References

1 Apple Podcasts Best practices, https://help.apple.com/itc/podcastsbestpractices/#/itcd55a9646a
2 Spotify for Artists FAQ, https://artists.spotify.com/faq/mastering-and-loudness#how-does-spotify-calculate-loudness
3 BBC Radio Commissioning technical specifications, https://downloads.bbc.co.uk/radio/commissioning/TechnicalSpecificationRadio.pdf
4 International Telecommunications Union Recommendation ITU-R BS.1770–4, https://www.itu.int/dms_pubrec/itu-r/rec/bs/R-REC-BS.1770-4-201510-I!!PDF-E.pdf

6   Publishing

Introduction to publishing

Let's be honest, the publishing part isn't much fun. It's also super nerve-wracking and very important. After all, what's the point of your lovingly crafted show if nobody hears it?

I get it, you didn't get into podcasting to fiddle around with web hosting platforms. You're tempted to just stick it on SoundCloud because if you build it, they will come, but you really need to get your show on to Spotify, Apple Podcasts and all the other places that people *actually listen to podcasts.*

Publishing properly is a really easy process, and as the industry flourishes loads of companies have popped up ready to help you get your show out there.

To publish a show, you need:

*   Your mastered MP3 file
*   Some artwork
*   A podcast hosting platform, which will provide a landing page and an Really Simple Syndication (RSS) feed

This final chapter is going to walk through that process so that your show is published properly and your potential adoring fans can find your show the same way they find any other podcast.

File formats

You've got your master WAV file, but that is way too big to stream online. When you click "save as", you are presented with a range of options.

There are a few formats you should know about, but Apple and Spotify's web player both deliver audio in Advanced Audio Coding (AAC) format.

Choosing the right file format is about balancing audio quality, file size and compatibility with different listening platforms. Most platforms allow users to set their own streaming quality now, so you might as well upload your podcast in the highest quality possible.

DOI: 10.4324/9781003046578-6

If we're being honest with ourselves, the majority of listeners aren't going to notice the difference between a 128kb/s MP3 and a full quality WAV once they are streaming your finished podcast. If you're looking to reach as many people as possible (and who isn't?), then compatibility should be your top priority.

So if all this looks like a lot to read, here's the tl;dr version: **work in WAV format as much as possible while you're making your podcast. Save a master copy in WAV, then convert it to MP3 at 128kb/s or higher to put the show online**.

Lossy vs lossless

File formats come in two types. Lossy files lose part of the original audio in order to save space. Lossless means all the original audio is preserved.

WAV

The big beast. The audio version of your photo negatives, HD film reel.

WAV files (sometimes pronounced wave) are your raw, uncompressed audio. This is the standard format for video and audio professionals to work in. You're an audio professional now, so you should work with this until it's time to upload your show too.

Some compression is supported by the WAV file format, but you aren't likely to run into that while making a podcast. If you see "PCM Wave", the PCM is Pulse Code Modulation and it is just referring to the format being uncompressed.

MP3

MPEG-Layer 3. The original gangster of lossy file formats. The one that started the streaming and file-sharing revolution by being small enough to send over the internet in those early days of dial-up modems. It's supported by pretty much every player, car stereo and phone operating system.

MP3s reduce or remove audio data that is usually outside what human hearing can perceive and uses efficient storage methods for the rest. An MP3 will be between 5% and 15% of the size of your uncompressed WAV. You can expect a half hour-long stereo show to be between 30MB and 70MB.

The quality of an MP3 file is measured by its bitrate, which goes up to 320kb/s.

The MP3 is everywhere, but it isn't perfect. The sharper eared listener will notice a loss in fidelity, especially in the top-end of the frequency spectrum. Once you drop below 256kb/s, you don't even need to be an audiophile to hear the difference in quality from a WAV file.

It's also not the best form of compressed audio. The main appeal of the MP3 is its ubiquity and near universal compatibility.

If you're ever given the option to save your MP3 in "constant bitrate" or "variable bitrate", use constant bitrate. Variable bitrate can shrink the file size some more but also cause problems on some players.

You can get 5.1 surround sound MP3s with certain encoding methods, but usually they are limited to stereo.

AAC

Advanced audio codec. The plucky upstart that's come along to challenge the MP3. While still using lossy compression, AAC is objectively the better format, with measurable differences in quality when using the same bitrate. It just sounds better while keeping similar file sizes to MP3.

This format was designed to be the successor to the MP3. It can accommodate up to 48 streams of audio at once.

It often appears as M4A. If you have done any remote recordings with someone using an iPhone, then you'll probably have received a file in this format.

Various parts of the industry are pushing AAC as the future of compressed audio. Apple Podcasts streams in AAC. Anchor, the simplified online podcast production service, outputs its files in AAC. Spotify's web player streams in AAC. It's plausible that AAC will eventually become the industry standard, but industry standards change slowly.

Right now though, MP3 is still the king. Spotify only accepts MP3s (even though they stream in AAC and OGG and they own Anchor which outputs AAC files), and they are one of the biggest listening platforms for podcasts.

If you go down the route of managing your feed entirely yourself, then you could plausibly upload your show to Spotify in MP3 and then to other platforms, such as Apple Podcasts in higher-quality M4A.

OGG

Vorbis OGG. The name comes from a Terry Pratchett novel. This is an open-source lossy file format that you are unlikely to receive any audio in, but you should know about anyway because it is the format Spotify's desktop and mobile apps stream in. It has higher fidelity than MP3 and generally similar to AAC, but is unrestricted by patents so software developers can use it more freely.

Other formats you might encounter

- **AIFF**: Audio Interchange File Format. Apple's version of WAV. It's virtually the same but less widely compatible and mostly used by producers who work in pro-tools.

- **WMA**: Windows Media Audio. Microsoft's audio format.
- **AMR**: Adaptive Multi-Rate codec. This was common in some older smartphones, so someone self-recording into one of these might send you something in AMR. It was designed to store spoken audio in small file sizes so they could be sent as voice notes. Unfortunately the priority was file size and intelligibility, not high-quality audio. When something arrives in AMR format, my heart sinks a little.

Spotify

Spotify's web player streams in AAC format at 128kb/s.[2]

The apps, whether on desktop or mobile, stream in Vorbis OGG at quality equivalent to bitrates of up to 320kb/s.

To submit to Spotify, your show needs to be in MP3 format between 96kb/s and 320kb/s. Your show can be a maximum of 200mb in size... but unless you're going over 80 minutes in length, then it will be under that even at 320kb/s[1]

It is a confusing mishmash of formats, and hopefully they'll standardise their file formats at some point, but until then, just remember to save it as an MP3 at a decent bitrate.

Apple podcasts

Apple are uncharacteristically a little less tyrannical on their file formats and will accept shows in MP3, AAC and some other formats not normally associated with audio that you shouldn't worry about (PDF anyone?).

AAC is Apple's chosen format for streaming in.

Google podcasts

Google doesn't appear to have any published guidelines on audio quality or format, so go ahead and reuse whatever you have submitted to Spotify and Apple.

That is an overwhelming amount of information when all you want to do is hit save and put your show on the internet. There are ways to get a podcast online in all the right places without thinking too much about file format: podcast hosting services that sort out all the backend of an RSS feed and submitting to the right places in the right format. Most professional producers use these rather than coding an RSS feed themselves.

What is an RSS feed?

RSS. Really Simple Syndication.

Or some people call it "rich site summary".

It's the core piece of internet technology that delivers podcasts. Even though podcasts are a new, exciting and booming industry, the simple

RSS feed that delivers them to listeners is a pretty outdated piece of tech. RSS feeds were never really mainstream; they are part of podcasting's nerdy origins that has stuck around and isn't going anywhere soon.

Before social media took over as the king of content aggregation, RSS feeds were a way to gather stripped-down versions of blogs, news articles and other regularly updated content in one place. They began as simple text files before evolving into code that could include images, videos and, crucially for us, audio.

The idea of an RSS feed is that a user can subscribe to the feed of various websites and their browser notifies them when a new piece of content is published, then they can read it directly from the feed in their browser or an RSS reader app. The user never has to actually go to the website they want to check.

This way of consuming content never fully took off though, and RSS readers fell out of favour. Google even discontinued Google Reader in 2013.

Now there is a different form of those early aggregation apps and websites: podcast player apps. Apple Podcasts, Stitcher, Google Podcasts... these are essentially just RSS feed readers with an audio player built in. These apps check the RSS feed for new episodes, downloads, streams or plays the audio file that the feed points to. They present the metadata of titles, artwork and descriptions in a properly designed interface.

The RSS feed is the way that a hosting platform where the podcast is actually stored interacts with a podcast library and player such as Apple Podcasts, so that a listener can open up their app and access the show.

The RSS feed itself is an extensible markup language (XML) file full of code and content. If you want to see an example of what it looks like under the hood, then check out *The Daily*'s RSS feed at http://rss.art19.com/the-daily.

For podcasts, the feed contains the code pointing towards the show's actual audio file as well as the following metadata:

- Title
- Description
- Artwork
- Category
- Language
- Explicit rating

It looks like it contains a lot, but really an RSS feed is just a tiny basic text file. The audio and image files have to be hosted separately and the RSS XML file just points to them.

As a producer, you really don't need to actually see inside that RSS file. It is a hidden piece of code that runs between the host and the podcast libraries.

Submit a podcast for publication

You're here. The finish line is in sight, you've made a podcast and the people need to hear it! Your adoring fans are waiting.

How on Earth do we get this thing on the internet? And not just on the internet, but available in all the places that people actually go to listen to podcasts, such as Spotify, Apple Podcasts and Google Podcasts.

In theory you could start a website and just host it on your own server; however, learning to code your RSS feed and then create a platform that people are actually going to visit requires at least one more book's worth of instruction, and even then your show wouldn't be available on Spotify.

Here's what you need before you are ready to publish your show:

- MP3 file
- Logo image
- A written description
- An RSS feed, generated by your hosting platform

You've already made the MP3 file, so let's sort out the rest.

Don't rush the logo and description. You spent all that time and creativity on the MP3, but this is probably the thing that people will see first as they browse looking for a podcast to listen to.

Logo image

This should be square (1:1 ratio) and at least 1400 × 1400 pixels, with a maximum of 3000 × 3000 pixels as either JPG or PNG. Those are Apple's specifications, and if you follow those, the other platforms will accept it too.

Description

It would be much easier if there was a fixed length that show what descriptions should be, but they get cut off at different points on different devices, usually between 120 and 160 characters. You should keep your descriptions short with the most important information at the start. That first sentence should draw a listener in and make them want to click on your show. If you are writing it longer than 130 characters or so, then you need to really give them a reason to click the "more" button.

Choosing a hosting platform

As the podcast industry has grown from a few enthusiasts with laptops and microphones to a booming international industry, a whole range of platforms have sprung up that handle the backend of podcast publishing. Some of them can even help you monetise your show.

When you sign up with a hosting platform, you are signing up for:

- Hosting the file online
- Bandwidth for listeners
- A "landing page", a simple website that your episodes are posted to
- An RSS feed of that landing page

Most importantly, they store your audio and generate the RSS feed for you. Once you've filled out all the fields and signed up for a hosting platform, you'll have a Uniform Resource Locator (URL) that you can copy and paste to the podcast libraries.

There are loads of them out there; the following is a short list of some of the most popular:

- **Libsyn** is pretty good for hosting a single podcast at a very low monthly rate and has a good customisable embed player.
- **Buzzsprout** is a common choice for newbie podcasters as it allows free hosting, although only up to two hours of audio per month with episodes disappearing after 90 days.
- **Acast** has free hosting, with paid plans if you want to monetise your show and add additional features.
- **Simplecast** is a little pricier but allows for managing lots of different podcasts with different team members for professional productions.
- **Anchor** is owned by Spotify and so has some integration; it is also designed to be the simplest, easiest and free platform still allowing for monetisation.

Some of these platforms have services to help you monetise your podcast, often involving them selling advertising space on your show and taking a cut of that advertising revenue.

Submitting your show to libraries

Once you've picked a hosting platform and created your RSS feed, you need to tell the various podcast libraries where to look for it.

Apple and Spotify might be the dominant ways that people listen to podcasts, but in order to maximise our listenership you want to appear in the following places at a minimum:

- **Apple Podcasts**

Format requirements: M4A (AAC), MP3. At least one episode.

Previously iTunes. Generally accepted as the most popular podcast app, probably due to its ubiquity in iPhones, although Spotify is hot on its heels. If you don't list yourself here, you're depriving yourself of a huge chunk of your audience.

You need an Apple ID for this. If you've ever used iTunes or an iPhone before, you probably have one. Once you submit a show with your Apple ID, you have to contact Apple in order to switch it to another user.

It can take up to a week for Apple to approve podcasts and they won't accept an RSS feed that doesn't already have an episode in it. In order to make sure that the first episode of a show is on Apple Podcasts, on launch date lots of producers also publish an "Episode 0", a trailer, which Apple will accept.

The actual process is super simple. You just log in to a website called "iTunes Connect", click the "podcasts" section and then paste your RSS feed URL in to the box and hit validate, then wait for it to be published.

- **Spotify**

Format requirements: MP3 between 92kb/s and 320kb/s. Maximum size 200mb.

Spotify is the second biggest platform and could well overtake Apple podcasts by the time you read this. They're investing huge amounts of money into podcasts; you want to be on Spotify.

It's a similar process to Apple, you just head to podcasters spotify.com and paste in your RSS URL, although you have to type in the description and image yourself.

- **Google Podcasts**

Format requirements: have your own website – most hosting platforms create a landing page that will fulfil this role.

Google Podcasts uses Google's web crawler technology to hunt down and index your podcast without you having to do anything, just wait a while. Once that has happened, you can claim your show by creating an account on their podcast manager at podcastsmanager.google.com

- **Stitcher**

Format requirements: at least one episode. Unique title.

Stitcher follows the same signup process as Apple and Spotify, just go to their signup form at https://partners.stitcher.com/ with your RSS URL handy.

Once you've done all these, a bunch of other platforms pull the show from them and your podcast is out there, falling freely from headphones to eardrums.

References

1 https://podcasters.spotify.com/terms/Spotify_Podcast_Delivery_Specification_v1.6.pdf
2 https://support.spotify.com/us/article/high-quality-streaming/

7 Jargon buster

Audio Interface: a device which plugs into a computer, usually via USB, which allows audio signals to be fed to the computer and for the computer to feed them back. Usually contains several XLR and TRS inputs as well as several outputs. May also be referred to as a sound card or an Analogue to Digital Converter (ADC).

Balanced: when referring to cables, this means the cable contains three pieces of wire: two signal wires and a ground wire. The sending equipment sends two signals. The signals are identical, except that one is the exact inverse of the other (out of phase). When the signal reaches the receiving equipment, it flips the inverted signal back. Any interference picked up along the way will have affected both signals, except the distortion is now out of phase on one signal and will cancel itself out, leaving us with a clean signal.

Bleed: when two mics are relatively close to each other so they pick up each others desired audio sources.

Condenser: a type of microphone that is more sensitive but requires phantom power.

Compressor: software or hardware designed to reduce the dynamic range of an audio signal.

DAW: Digital Audio Workstation. Audio editing software such as Adobe Audition, Pro Tools, Audacity or Logic.

Destructive Editing: editing an audio file directly as opposed to non-destructive editing which is usually used in multitracks and edits clips that alter how the file is played back.

deciBels: the standard measurement of how loud a signal is. When working digitally, this will be dBfs – for deciBels full scale. That means that 0 is the absolute maximum. dBfs is a relative scale and is used digitally because it doesn't refer to any real physical property. It is purely numbers that are expressing the difference between two values, in this case amplitudes.

DeciBels are logarithmic meaning that 8dB is not double the loudness of 4dB. Perceived loudness does not increase in a linear fashion. An increase of 10dB is equivalent to a doubling of perceived loudness.

DOI: 10.4324/9781003046578-7

If you're working with hardware, then it may be in deciBel units (dBu) or decibel Volts (dBV) and these can go above zero. dBu and dBv are designed for measuring voltage and refer to an actual physical property.

DeEsser: a type of compressor that only applies to a narrow band, designed to remove over-emphasised sibilants.

Diaphragm: the piece of metal within a microphone that is moved by soundwaves. Think of it like your microphone's version of an eardrum.

Double-Ender: a remote recording where two separate recordings are made to be synced up later. Usually a double-ender features the interviewee recording themselves with a smartphone or their own recording device.

Dynamic: a type of microphone that is less sensitive, doesn't require phantom power and is often cheaper than condenser microphones.

Dynamic Range: the difference between the loudest possible signal and the quietest.

EQ or Equaliser: software or hardware which can cut or boost bands within the frequency spectrum.

Equal Gain: a type of crossfade made up of two linear fades. The simplest type of crossfade, but can create the impression of a dip in level in the centre of the fade.

Equal Power: a type of crossfade that sounds natural to the human ear.

Gain: amplification control applied to an incoming signal. Can be used to amplify or decrease amplification.

Hz or Hertz: cycles per second. In audio this is referring to frequency content and is usually between bass frequencies down to 20Hz and treble frequencies up to 20,000Hz, the range of human hearing.

ID3 Tags: metadata which adds artwork, genre and show descriptions to an MP3.

KHz or KiloHertz: 1KHz is 1,000Hz.

Line Level: −10dBV. This is the level at which audio equipment is calibrated to and roughly the level that a microphone signal is boosted to by a preamp.

LUFS or LKFS: Loudness Units Full Scale. The standard measurement for determining how loud audio is over an extended period of time.

Mastering: the act of creating the final "master" copy of a podcast.

Mic Level: the unamplified signal from a microphone, usually too low to use without passing through a preamp.

Monitors: in audio this refers to a type of studio speaker which aims not to colour the sound at all, providing an accurate listening experience for the producer and engineer.

Non-Destructive Editing: editing audio without altering the underlying file. Common in multitracks which use clips to alter the way a file is played back. This is as opposed to destructive editing which alters the audio file directly.

Pan: a control to change the balance between left and right of a stereo signal.

Phantom Power: the power, at +48 volts, required for a condenser microphone to operate.

Plug-In: a piece of software that appears within your DAW. These are often effects processors, bought or downloaded separately from your main editing software and then installed into it.

Preamp: the amplifier which sits between a microphone and recording equipment, such as a computer. Often these are built into an audio interface.

Reverb: simulated echoes or reverberations.

RSS Feed: the internet technology which distributes podcasts to podcast libraries such as Spotify or iTunes.

Sibilants: "sss" sounds in speech, which can sometimes sound harsh.

Tape Sync: similar to a double ender, except usually used to refer to a remote recording where a producer/engineer has been hired in the guest's location to make a professional recording.

Top and Tail: cutting an interview just to the start and end of the recorded interview, without doing any internal edits.

TRS: Tip Ring Sleeve, often referred to as a jack. This is the standard audio jack that you see on headphones. Comes in 1/4 inch and 1/8 inch sizes. This is balanced, meaning that they are resistant to interference. There are two types of TRS connector: plug and socket, although a lot of more old fashioned literature and engineers refer to these as male and female jacks.

Wildtrack: a recording of only the atmospheric sound taken from the same location as an interview, to be used in editing.

XLR: a type of connector on an audio cable. These are the standard type of cabling for microphones and a lot of other professional audio gear. They're balanced, meaning that they are resistant to interference. There are two types of XLR connector: plug and socket, although a lot of more old fashioned literature and engineers refer to these as male and female XLRs.

Index

Note: Page numbers in *italic* indicate illustrations.